book reviews

The reader feels like he or she is having a friendly chat about herbs. Martin's slight sardonic sense of humor entertains the reader on a topic which could be a bit dry. Her directions are easy to follow… tone and style are comfortable and easy to read. Her techniques are unique and convenient for use by nearly anyone. It is obvious she has used the techniques extensively and has put a lot of research and time into this book. Quality shows.

Eileen Troemel
www.FacingNorth.net

I would definitely recommend this book to anyone interested in working with herbs. It is written in a style that is appealing to many different levels of experience.

Dawn Thomas
www. globalgoddess.org/oracle

This is exactly the kind of book that I want to see more of–not rehashes of the same old stuff, a bunch of reworked Culpeper and Cunningham. In this book, we get an innovative collection of ideas with enough information to effectively put them into practice, but without a bunch of fluff and filler. In short–this is an awesome book, and I can't recommend it enough.

Lupa
greenwolf.com

readers respond

This is such an informative book, and beautifully formatted and illustrated.

J'Ann Alvarado

A wonderful book. Not just a reference for herbs and their usage, but a work of art, too. What a great addition to my herbal library.

Len Ellis

I love your "Spirit Herbs" book. It's really great and so well put together. I was excited to see that you included the information about salt -- so important! The illustrations and pictures are so well done, the charts and recipes are great and easy to use. It's really a joy to work with. I love it! Being able to look up an individual herb in the detailed compendium and finding not only its botanical name and aroma but also its planetary ruler, element and sexuality. The different blends you have created makes this book a breeze to use everyday.

Linda Petty

Spirit Herbs: Simple Recipes for Hibachi Herbal Magic & Sacred Space

published by

moonlady media

www.Moonlady.com

381 Casa Linda Plaza, box 137, Dallas, Texas 75218
moonladymedia@sbcglobal.net

SAN: 8 5 6 – 7 0 2 6

ISBN 10: 0-9818424-0-2
ISBN 13: 978-0-9818424-0-0

Library of Congress Control Number

First Printing July 2008

Printed in the United States of America

table of contents

the resources

preface

gratitude

I am grateful to the members of the Moonlady Community in North Texas for their energy and support, and to the many hundreds of people who have attended my seasonal events and been the test subjects for several of these blends. I am also grateful to the women of the Goddess Creative, New Moon and Women's Well list serves (especially Barbara Ardinger) for their encouragement of my writing. But most of all I am grateful to my husband Scooter Smith for his support and impeccable work designing, illustrating and laying out this book.

please don't steal this book

Many hours of work and a significant investment of money went into the creation, research, writing, editing, layout and production of this book. Please do not reproduce this book or use the contents as if they were your own. No matter how you try to justify it, it's not a morally acceptable thing to do. If you do steal this book, may Ix Chel crash your crown chakra. You won't be happy about it; she can be an ornery crone! For use of excerpts from this book, please contact Moonlady Media.

disclaimers

Here's the part where I tell you things that are simple common sense.

Disclaimer #1

Use common sense. This book assumes you have some. The author cannot be held liable for your lack of common sense.

Disclaimer #2

Don't burn yourself up. The Hibachi Herbal Magic techniques outlined in this book incorporate lighter fluid, self-lighting charcoal and butane lighters. Exercise caution when using these flammable items. Read and follow all cautions outlined in all chapters.

Disclaimer #3

Don't burn everybody else up. Hibachi Herbal Magic is not for parties.

Disclaimer #4

Inhaling the smoke of some herbs described in this book may impair judgment. After ingesting these herbs, which are noted as such in the text, do not drive vehicles, perform complex tasks or operate large machinery. Just chill. Read and follow all cautions contained in the text.

Disclaimer #5

If you have respiratory issues, do not inhale the fumes of charcoal when it is being ignited or the smoke of burning herbs. Read and follow all cautions contained in the Hibachi 101 and Burning Herbs section.

introduction

I am an herb junkie. As a pre-teen in the tamped down WASP-nirvana that was Dallas in the sixties, I was totally enamored with the herbal shampoo from Clairol, a marketing nod to the hippies of the era. To this day, if I see "herb" in a description at a restaurant I'll order the dish. All my soaps, shampoos and such have some aroma to them and the first thing I do in my office in the morning is turn on the essential-oil diffuser.

It's worse than that. I buy herbs I'll never use, just because they're cool. How can you resist boldo? It's supposed to have quite a buzz, but I've never had the nerve to try it. I had small jars of High John the Conqueror and Jacob's Ladder just because I like esoteric herbs with Biblical names. But I finally had to cut back my herb hoarding to free up cabinet space for important things like food.

That herbal purging had its upside. I had to test and evaluate which herbs were effective and which were just cool. Those ceremonial herbs that remained constitute an herbal library that anyone can manage. Many are considered simple kitchen spices. I take great pleasure in herbs and want to bring some of that to you.

SECTION MENU

sacred space

If you want to adjust or amplify the energy of a indoor space, you can place a crystal here and a sacred object there, perhaps do a little feng shui with fountains and chimes. Voila! But it's not so easy outside, especially if you have limited money to invest and just need a temporary sacred space setting for a ceremony in a public park.

During my nearly two decades of presenting ceremonies, I've found that many herbs are excellent at holding and affecting certain energies, even in their raw, unaltered state. Plus, herbs have two side benefits. They're often quite cheap and smell very good. Perfect qualities for outdoor use!

The right blend of herbs strewn about or placed in strategically located containers can absorb or deflect unpleasant energy and transform a common place into sacred space. On altars and in ceremonies, herbs are able to carry powerful, prayerful intent.

hibachi herbal magic

For smudging, most folks turn to the trusty smudge stick, a long tied-up bundle of dried leafy herb stems, usually sage. As a gentle smudge for individuals, this is great and it's especially handy for indoor use. For smudging a group, however, you're in for a long wait to smudge each and every person individually. Traditionally the smudge stick has to be waved over both sides of each person's body, plus their head, hands and feet.

In ceremony, this slow motion smudge-a-thon can be a real energy deflator with bored people standing around waiting. And the smudge can be, well, wimpy. In Hibachi Herbal Magic, loose herbs are tossed on hot charcoal, producing billows of aromatic smoke. It's a whole-body immersion smudge that takes an instant. Mayans have done it this way for centuries. With new advances in charcoal and lighter fluid, hibachis can be easy to light and ecological, too.

Burning herbs in ceremonies as an offering can be just as potent. The smoke makes manifest the elements of both air and fire, highlighting their turbulent and fluid power in a dramatic way. The aromas released can have a powerful effect on the mind and heart. The smoke carries prayers and other intentions heavenward, with each herb creating a different personality of smoke.

who am I?

People in North Texas call me the Moonlady for my 2750+ member eclectic/holistic/spiritual list serve called Moonlady News. My website, www.moonlady.com, is home to the News and Moonlady Media, the publisher of this booklet. The popular SkyCycles page, with its collection of lunar and seasonal calendars, is also based there.

The recipes and how-to knowledge in this book come from over fifteen years of presenting public seasonal ceremonies and group rituals in Dallas. I've led many women's circles and other ensembles, been guest ceremonialist at numerous conferences and retreats, and produced Summer Solstice events that have attracted over 2000+ people.

Currently, I'm best known for my Winter SolstiCelebrations, now in their 16th year and attended by 750 to 1000 folks each December, plus Moonlady Fests at White Rock Lake held near the Spring and Fall Equinoxes. I'm founder and executive director of Earth Rhythms [www.EarthRhythms.org], which presents experiential events, preserves natural places, and provides help to those in need in North Texas.

I've been a Taoist since a teenager, seeing in nature the wisdom required for living a good life, and was blessed to have much rural experience growing up. My husband Scooter and I are transforming a set of decrepit farms into a nature preserve northeast of Dallas, turning pastures into prairies and bringing health back to woodlands besieged by invasive non-native plants. I hope to have the herb garden of my dreams out there someday.

how to use this book

This book was written for people who want to work with herbs, particularly in groups, but need to keep it simple. It's like a recipe book. Look up what you want to do, such as a group smudge, take down the information needed, and go to the store or web site. Then simply prepare, mix and enjoy the blends.

The book's first section features short how-to chapters on working with herbs, dealing with hibachis, and the art of starting a charcoal fire. The second section contains recipes for burning and strewing herbs. The concluding section contains a descriptive compendium of herbs used in the recipes, plus sources for herbs and resources for further study.

Smudges provide a supremely effective method to shift from the mundane to the sacred. There is immense power in purifying, empowering smudges and the giving of symbolic substances as burnt offerings. These burning herbs can connect you to the divine in a most dramatic and aromatic way. Strewing herbs to create sacred space ties you to traditions going back thousands of years. With this book, actions formerly relegated to priests, priestesses and those with in-depth study can now easily be yours.

ritual use of herbs

strewing ~ burning ~ intent

The ritual use of herbs involves their effect on the mind and spirit, rather than the body as in health and beauty herbalism. Because rituals are often performed in groups, using herbs can present real challenges. Smudging a few hundred people can be quite an operation! Group activities often mean meeting in public spaces, which present another round of issues in site preparation. Try holding a contemplative ceremony in a park after a rugby match – that's quite an onerous and inebriated energy to overcome!

This book focuses on two group techniques for the ritual use of herbs: burning and strewing. Both should be performed with spiritual intent.

SECTION MENU

strewing

Strewing – a nice word for tossing herbs about – is easiest. No equipment, just a jar of herbs and your hands. Strewing connotes a light but thorough scattering. It excels when you're outside, where the herbs' energies can meld so well with those of the Earth. Strewing is an easy way to involve others in the site preparation, as long as they strew with the proper intent.

Strewing is great for changing the energy of a place and instilling a positive charge

right, the author begins to create a sacred space with strewing

right, creating a sacred space with strewing that measures 3 to 5 feet out from the edge of the hibachi (which is placed close to vegetation for photographic purposes only)

with herbs known to absorb or deflect negative energy. You can prepare a place for dancing, drumming, or communing more deeply at a sacred site with herbs that help connect your energy to the Earth. Or create a secure perimeter for a ceremony site with a blend of herbs that protect.

The focus of the book is on the outdoor use of herbs, but the strewing blends are also applicable for indoors. Since tossing herbs inside a house, business or rented facility isn't always kosher, I've included herbs in bowls and other containers. Or indoor strewing can be followed by a thorough sweeping or vacuuming.

burning

Smudging affects the energetic body, our aura or "vibe" that extends invisibly from our physical body. We give our corporeal bodies frequent baths, why not bathe our energetic body as well? It's our outer layer of defense against the outside world and works hard to deflect the negativity and stress. Spiff up and soothe your vibe!

In my Hibachi Herbal Magic method, loose herbs are tossed on a hibachi of hot charcoal. Great clouds of smoke arise that thoroughly smudge you. To smudge a group of people all they have to do is stand downwind! Or people can smudge themselves individually and control how much smoke they want. You can even straddle the hibachi and get really smudged! The hibachi method of smudging is great for purifying large objects such as staffs and cloaks before ceremonial use.

Burnt offerings – the placing of sacred herbs on hot embers – can be a powerful ceremonial method. It represents a way to give up something important as an act of humility to the divine, much as animal sacrifices were once used. But burnt offerings are far nicer! When made with dense resins and woods they produce a heavy smoke with an unfolding multilayered aroma. The aroma of burned herbs can be incredibly transportive, taking those who inhale to great mental and spiritual states. Inhalants are herbal blends that are burned for aromas that affect the mental state, but are not performed with spiritual intent.

Combining these methods and going a step beyond is the immersant, an intense smudging done naked or lightly clothed with the intent of altering consciousness. Part of the immersant's impact is its aroma and part is the herb's active constituents being inhaled and absorbed into your skin. The effect of immersion, however, is shorter lasting than if the herbs were ingested. Immersion is for private individual and small group adult ceremonies only.

intent

It's easy to say that if you use this herb you'll be purified or protected. Or smell this and you'll reach nirvana. But the magic is not solely in the herbs, just as an icon of a goddess is not the goddess herself. You are the conduit for earthly and universal energies. When they are used with spiritual intent, herbs can serve as a powerful focusing lens.

Visualizing, chanting and incanting are helpful to attain an intentional mindframe. Always be aware of where you are in relation to the directions, and move clockwise when you want to send energy outward and counterclockwise to bring energy inward. Prime yourself to be a conduit of energy by using yoga or tai chi to tap into the upward waves of magnetism and the downward attraction of gravity. As you strew herbs or use them in other ways, be aware of your breath and stay true to who you are.

herbal 101

where to buy herbs
how to measure and store
preparing and blending herbs

Working with ceremonial herbs for burning and strewing is like cooking or chemistry. Simple elemental building blocks are combined and catalyzed into something well beyond the individual parts.

types of ceremonial herbs

The word "herb" may bring to mind the little flecks of green in your marinara or salsa. But herbs go well beyond leaves and stems. Ceremonial herbs include flowers (so friendly), seeds, berries and buds (potently concentrated), bark and wood (rough and primeval), roots (mysterious and uber-powerful), and resins and saps (fantastic powerful aromas).

Bark & Wood

Most wood has a diffuse but solid energy that carries the metaphorical qualities of the trunk of a tree: bringing the light of Sun and the dark of Earth into a core of strength. Inner or outer layers of bark are used and come in a wide variety of textures. It takes a high heat to ignite wood and bark, and the smoke (except for sandalwood and a few others) tends to be harsh, though the aroma of the plant carries forward nicely. Always grind wood well before strewing or burning.

Leaves
The herbiest parts of herbs are the leaves, the green blend of Earth and Sun energy that celebrates photosynthesis and the great pranic breath of the planet. The aroma of burning leaves is often quite different from what they smell like fresh or dried. Use the lowest heat possible to burn leaves. Crush between your fingers while strewing to release the aroma.

Resins & Saps
Resins are the most elite of ceremonial herbs and the priciest as well. Sap is a fluid that moves through trees, such as maple syrup in maple trees. In some trees, like frankincense, the extracted sap dries into a heavy, dense resin for burning as incense. Similar methods are used to create a gum extract or resin. When derived from sacred woods, these represent the blood of the tree. Inhale the burning fragrance and be in communion with the World Tree from which humankind developed.

But do remember that resins are heavy with natural hydrocarbons. (After all, turpentine is made from pine sap.) Resins will flame up when tossed on embers. Toss on too many and you'll find yourself with a rowdy fire. I once packed a Yule Log with resins that sent horizontal flames shooting out two feet when the log was lit during the ceremony. The hem of my long dress caught on fire in front of 200 folks who were both horrified and highly entertained by the little pyro-dance I did to put it out.

Roots
I love roots, so earthy, raw and resplendent with dark power. Larger tuberous roots, when fresh, can even be a pleasant chew, but the dried pieces are tough and hard to grind. Be prepared to beat and chop on them a bit first. Roots don't strew or burn effectively until they've been ground to a rough powder.

Seeds, Berries & Buds
These fertile capsules hold a concentrated energy and represent poised potential. Crush, burn or brew to release their full aroma.

buying herbs

Bulk herbs can be found at many natural food stores, though the focus in grocery stores is usually on edible ones. Some alternative, counterculture and garden shops also carry them. To find a full array of herbs, metaphysical stores, especially those with a pagan bent, are your best bet. But unless you're in a big city, or in hip areas of the West or East Coast or the Rocky Mountains, retail herbal pickings can be slim.

If you cannot find a good local herb store, or need specialized herbs, go online. The following vendors have great policies, including carrying organic herbs when possible and nothing that's ever been sprayed. Their wild herbs are sustainably harvested.

Frontier	**www.frontiercoop.com**	The big kahuna, stunningly wide variety, big quantities, fast service.
Living Earth	**www.livingearthherbs.com**	The new quality kid in town and trying hard to do right, passionate about plants.
Mountain Rose	**www.mountainroseherbs.com**	Big on quality and care, a botanical wonderland run by plant geeks.

Of course, growing your own in an herb garden is the best way of all. I love taking a deep snort of fresh dill or lavender; the relaxation is so quick and deep.

weighing & measuring

Most leafy herbs sold come already cut and sifted, which means the leaves were sliced into small squares and dried, then sifted to remove small stems. Bark, wood and resin come in chunks or shreds. All also come ground into a powder. But the more intact the herb is, the fresher it will be, so buy whole when you can and grow your own when possible. I prefer white sage that has been lightly chopped, leaving bundles of leaves on stem ends that make terrific smudge sticks.

Herbs are generally sold by weight, usually ounces, not by volume. Few folks have an accurate scale around the house, so the recipes in this book are given in dry-weight cup measurements as well as by ratio.

Here are some approximate volume-to-dry weight correlations to use when purchasing herbs:

Approximate Volume-To-Dry Weight Correlations

Barks & Woods	1 cup = 2 ounces
Leaves & Flowers	1 cup = 1 ounce
Roots	½ cup = 2.5 ounces
Sap & Resin Powders	¼ cup = 1 ounce
Sap & Resin Chunks	½ cup = 2.5 ounces
Seeds, Buds & Berries	½ cup = 1.5 ounces

These are average conversions. Small leaves such as thyme will settle more densely and weigh more by volume, as will resin-heavy ones like rosemary. Hairy or fluffy leaves don't settle as much and will weigh less. Little flowers like elder will settle, while larger ones such as hops will not.

Seeds, buds, berries, barks, woods and roots are much heavier than leaves. Saps and resins are the heaviest of all. The same rule applies. Denser, smaller and more finely chopped herbs will weigh more by volume.

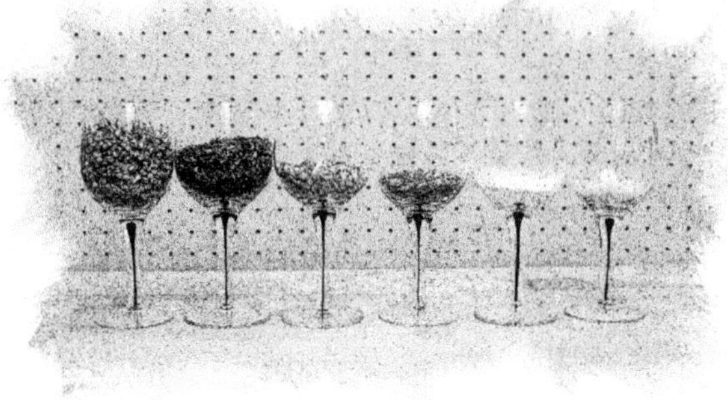

above left: from left to right, an ounce each of flowers, leaves, roots, bark, powder and resin

above right: an ounce of coltsfoot (left) comnpared to an ounce of thyme

preparing herbs

When buying herbal equipment, avoid plastic, wood and other materials that absorb aromas.

Measuring

For making these herb recipes you'll need cups used to measure dry things. (Glass cups are used for liquids.) They usually come as a nesting set of 1, 1/2, 1/3, and 1/4 cups. Look for sets that also have 1/8 cup, which is two tablespoons. You'll also need a nesting set of measuring spoons in 1 tablespoon and 1, 1/2, 1/4 and 1/8 teaspoons.

above left: nesting set of 1, 1/2, 1/3, and 1/4 cups (Yep, they're plastic, but it was the only full set we had to photograph.)

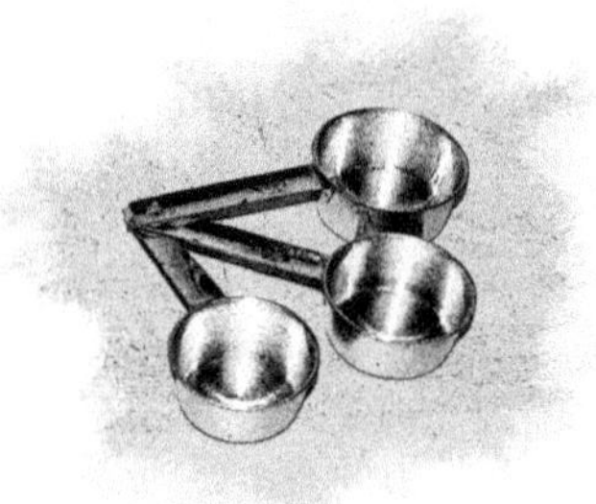

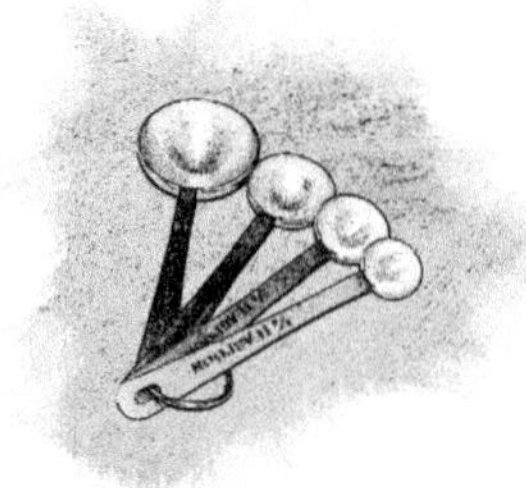

left and right: measuring sets ranging from 2 tbsp. to 1/8 tsp.

A scale can be very helpful as some people prefer to work in weights rather than measures. I use a digital postal scale that is accurate to a half ounce. There are much better quality scales out there; I'm just cheap. Folks into precision prefer a triple-beam scale.

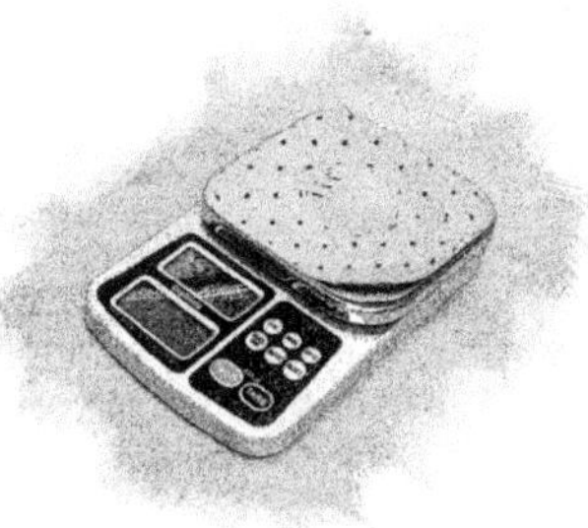

digital postal scale

Grinding

Herbal blends need to be a uniform texture so they will burn and broadcast evenly. Some will have to be ground first, either in an electric grinder or by using a mortar and pestle or manual chopper.

manual chopper

Wood, bark, root and sometimes saps usually need grinding. Gnarlier and harder chunks may require hands-on processing first lest they jam up your grinder. Break such sturdy herbs into smaller pieces by wrapping in a sturdy cotton cloth and whacking away at them with a hammer. Cheesecloth works, but I prefer canvas or one-sided terrycloth. Cloth diapers and napkins also work well. Bark and root can sometimes be cut with large scissors or chopped with a cleaver or large knife – if done carefully!

Almost any food or even coffee bean grinder will do for herbs. Mine is a basic pint-sized Cuisinart. Dedicate the grinder to herbs because you'll never get the smell out. After 10 years, my Cuisinart has become a tannish sage green with a most indefinable aroma; it's like chai tea combined with a garden salad, which smells better than that sounds. The electric grinding process kicks up a lot of dried herb dust, so run the kitchen exhaust fan or toss a towel over the grinder when you're working.

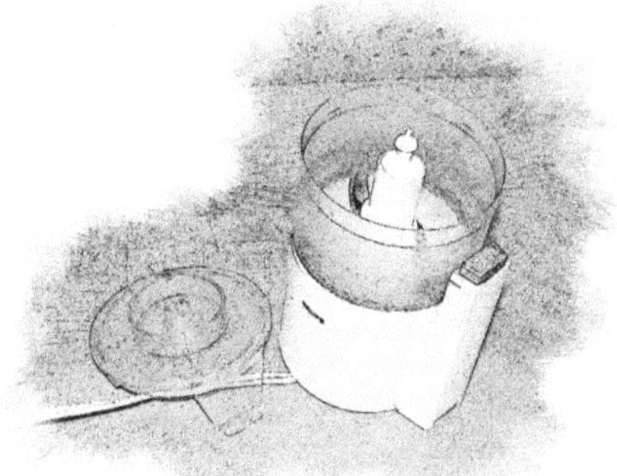

The classic marble mortar and pestle works for small amounts or softer herbs.

above: small food processor

left: mortar and pestle

Reconstituted stone is preferred since it will not

have cracks as natural stone often does. You can occasionally find brass sets. A hand chopper used to mince vegetables can also work for softer herbs.

Seeds and flowers don't usually need grinding unless large. Even then, be very careful not to over-grind; use manual methods rather than an electric grinder.

Blending

Once the herbs have been ground, you'll need a bowl to blend them in. Being inert and non-reactive, ceramic or glass bowls are best, but watch for cracks that can fill up with ground herbs. Stainless steel usually works just fine, but it can react with some resins, salts and other substances. Get a big enough metal serving spoon that can both stir the herbs and scoop into their storage containers. If you use bowls with snap-on lids, you can simply shake them to blend the herbs.

storing herbs

The two key words to remember for storing dried herbs are dark and cool. Sunlight and heat encourage herbs to release their volatile chemicals. A closet or cabinet is always best for storage. I can tell how serious a store is about their herbs by the way they display them. Arrayed on shelves in the front room looks good, but damages the herbs; tucked away in a dimly lit back room with no windows is preferred. Humidity is not good for herbs either, so avoid storing in the kitchen and bath, though you can use an humidity-absorbing system like Damp-Rid. As long as the containers are sealed super tight, your refrigerator or freezer works for long-term storage.

Glass containers are superior to plastic, which absorbs herbal aromas and lets in air. It's hard to beat the good old Mason jars, the kind used for home canning. The lid has a rubber gasket that enables you to screw it down tight, and when the rubber gets old you can just buy a new lid. Most large grocery stores will carry Mason jars and supplies. Ceramic canisters keep out light, but I prefer glass jars so I'm able to see what's in there.

storage jars with a variety lids

If you must go with plastic bags because of space, double bag or use dual-lined freezer bags. Or invest in a vacuum-pack system storage system used for food.

Label everything. I can't function without my Brother labelmaker (found in office supply stores). Write-on labels also work, but try to find water-resistant labels and use a Sharpie or other waterproof pen.

equipment list

Storage

double-walled plastic bags
glass jars
humidity-absorbing system like Damp-Rid
labelmaker
water-resistant labels & waterproof pen

Preparation

electric grinder
chopper
cotton cloth
hammer
measuring cups and spoons
mortar and pestle
scale

Blending

ceramic, glass or metal bowl
non-slotted metal serving spoon

hibachi 101

charcoal basics ~ the art of fire lighting
eco-alternatives ~ staying safe

To smudge or make a fire offering, toasty hot charcoal is required. The familiar little self-lighting charcoal discs are just too wimpy. You need real heat, the kind that barbeque charcoal can provide.

SECTION MENU

- *Burning Container*
- *Charcoal*
- *Ignition Methods*
- *Safety & Fire Tools*
- *Fire Making Skills*
- *Extinguishing Hot Charcoal*
- *Cautions*
- *Equipment List*

burning container

Hibachis

Hibachi is the Japanese word for "fire bowl." While it may be the quintessential apartment balcony barbeque grill, the classic round hibachi is perfect for burning herbs. A lid with adjustable vent holes is very helpful. Put it on the hibachi with the holes open to preserve hot charcoal between uses. Close the holes to reduce oxygen and extinguish the coals. Some hibachis even have handles, a big bonus.

My favorite is the classic Smokey Joe line from Weber [www.weber.com]. Lightweight with one long handle to keep you away from the heat, this squatty black porcelain-enameled steel hibachi is about 17 inches tall and 15 inches across. The round bowl has air-intake holes in the bottom and the lid has adjustable vent holes that create the airflow necessary for a good fire. It does get very hot, but cools off fast.

Smokey Joe is great for smudging because you can get up close. Straddle the hibachi to smudge the goods! It also has a tripod leg system, which evokes the classic cauldron. The larger One-Touch line sits about a yard high and two of the legs have wheels for easy moving. It's good for offerings and inhalants, but not smudges or immersants. Either of these hibachis will run you $30 to $40.

Weber Smoky Joe

Weber One Touch

Cast-iron has the advantage of being very stable, and the disadvantage of being heavy to carry and slow to cool. Cheap rectangular cast-iron hibachis often sold in department stores are just too shallow to handle herb burning well at all. For the best in cast-iron units seek out the oval Sportsman's Grill by Lodge [www.lodgemfg.com] with its nice deep charcoal well. A low-riding 8 inches high, which makes it very stable, it's about 9 inches wide and 20 inches long. The cost is about $100, but a cast-iron unit will last forever.

Fire Pits

Portable metal fire pits work fine, especially for offerings, and some are quite stunning. Certainly if looks is what you want, a fire pit is your choice. But getting close enough to the larger ones for a good smudging or immersion can be a challenge. Most are on handy wheels. Expect to pay $100 or more for a good one.

Chimneas

A chimnea is an enclosed fire pit with a vertical chimney and an opening on the side to insert firewood. Most chimneas are made of pottery, but occasionally metal ones can be found. Because the chimney directs the smoke upward from four to six feet, chimneas are suitable for burning offerings and inhalants, but not for smudges and immersants because the smoke must make body contact.

Pottery

A terra cotta clay garden pot can serve as a charcoal-burning container as long as it's about 1/3 inch thick and unglazed. A wide and relatively shallow shape works best because it creates more hot surface area and allows for better air motion. The drainage hole facilitates some air intake if the pot is set on an elevated non-flammable grid. These pots will eventually crack from the heat and make a big mess, but they are cheap to replace.

Portable Units

Sometimes a hibachi is just too big and a smaller, more portable unit is needed. The units described below can be used with barbeque charcoal. They produce significantly more smoke than a smudge stick, but less than a hibachi. They work great for intimate outdoor events and can be taken indoors for a brief smudging as long as no birds are present and the rooms are well ventilated afterward. Once ignited, barbeque charcoal releases small amounts of carbon monoxide.

cast iron censer

A censer is a metal or stone container used to hold hot charcoal for burning incense and herbs; they are sometimes filled with sand first. Censers can look really cool! When suspended from a chain, as typically seen in Catholic ceremonies, it's called a thurible. The suspending chain can get dang hot! Make sure you get a thurible that can stand erect when you set it down on a surface.

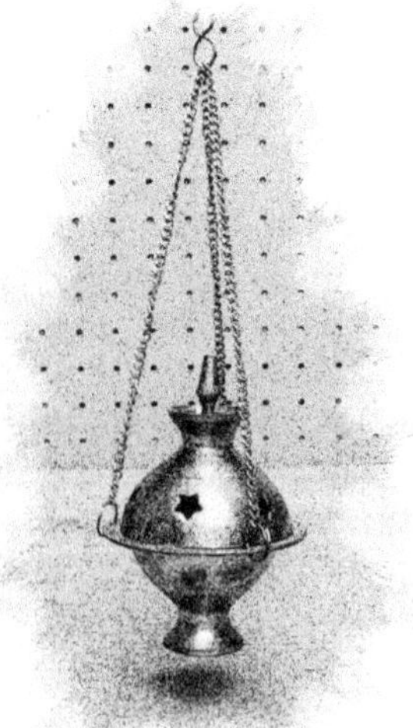

thurible

Indigenous Mesoamerican and Mayan ceremonies often feature a large terra cotta clay chalice that holds two to three cups or embers and is porous enough to dissipate heat quickly. Such chalices range from simple to ornate. A miniature chimnea, usually about 10 inches high, is very similar and quite portable.

terra cotta chalice

These units are too cramped to start barbeque charcoal in; it took a couple of ceremonial embarrassments before I figured that out. Instead, fill the unit with embers from a separate fire. Another option is to fill the unit with a dozen or more self-lighting charcoal disks.

charcoal

Charcoal comes in three main flavors: lump, natural and briquettes.

Lump Charcoal

Old-timey charcoal, aka lump charcoal or charwood, is created by charring, which is the burning of wood in a low-oxygen setting. The wood turns into black, brittle, porous chunks of 90 percent or more carbon. It's almost like coal and lights easily.

But lump charcoal is not an ecological choice unless you use something certified by the Rainforest Alliance's SmartWood program. Lump charcoal made by Noram de Mexico is charred from sustainably harvested oak hardwood and is available at some Sam's and Mexican grocery stores. Lazzari [www.lazzari.com] is an ecological brand that uses mesquite, an aggressive tree that can be invasive to ecosystems. The mesquite smell, while great for barbeque, can interfere with herbal aromas.

Natural Charcoal

Natural charcoal, which is usually made from recycled wood and timber, is more environmentally sound. It's easy to find in eco or health-food stores and is gaining wider distribution. Because most natural charcoal burns cooler, it is preferred for leaf blends. It goes to embers faster, but also burns out faster. The pieces are often flat, which holds the herbs better. And it's generally cheap.

Some new brands of natural charcoal use extrusion manufacturing. Wood waste and other organic matter are fused under high pressure and extruded into shapes that are then charred, or the source material is pre-charred. Extrusion charcoal burns hotter and lasts longer. Greenlink Charcoal All Natural Briquettes [www.greenlinkcharcoal.com] use waste wood and coconut shells with a natural food-grade binder. Greenlink also offers Coconut Shell Briquette Charcoal. Black Pearl [www.blackpearlcharcoal.com] is another line of coconut shell charcoal.

The bugaboo of natural charcoal is ignition; it's more challenging to light than lump charcoal, but easier than briquettes. This is a Boy Scout art for sure. Essential lighting info is given in the Ignition Methods section below. Or try One Light Charcoal [http://www.onelightcharcoal.com], natural charcoal pre-packed in a burnable bag. Light the ignition stick and let it go. The bag burns away, leaving behind a pile of hot charcoal.

Charcoal Briquettes

Charcoal briquettes, made by pressing wood waste and saw dust with an industrial binder, usually plant starch, are the most common charcoal. Accelerants like nitrate are added to help ignition and limestone is mixed in so that the coals turn white when ready. But even more crap can get put into lesser brands of briquettes including coal dust and toxic minerals. The FDA does not require that charcoal ingredients be listed, so you're best sticking with big brands like Match Light. Self-lighting briquettes are saturated with petroleum solvents.

Briquettes burn hotter than natural charcoal, making them good for root blends. They stand up to cold weather better and last longer, but they also take a while to cool down to proper embers. Herbs tend to slide off the embers unless the curved briquettes are crushed. Like lump and natural charcoal, you supply the ignition method.

Self-lighting briquettes are the easiest, most foolproof method. Build a pyramid of briquettes in a container, light it and come back in 20 minutes to hot coals. If you're working in a park or rural area, briquettes are easy to pack in. Just pre-load your burner with charcoal and head on out.

But there are downsides to self-lighting charcoal. It produces a big petrochemical stink and a hefty amount of air pollution when being lit. Fresh coals will have a faint residual smell from starter fluid that can interfere with herbal aromas. You can toss cedar wood shavings on the embers to help burn off the remaining chemmies.

ignition methods

A long wand lighter, also called a utility or candle lighter, is a must. Some pagans term it the "Sacred Bic." Or use long fireplace matches. Keep at least 8 inches between your hand and the hibachi when you're igniting the charcoal, especially self-lighting briquettes which tend to flame up fast.

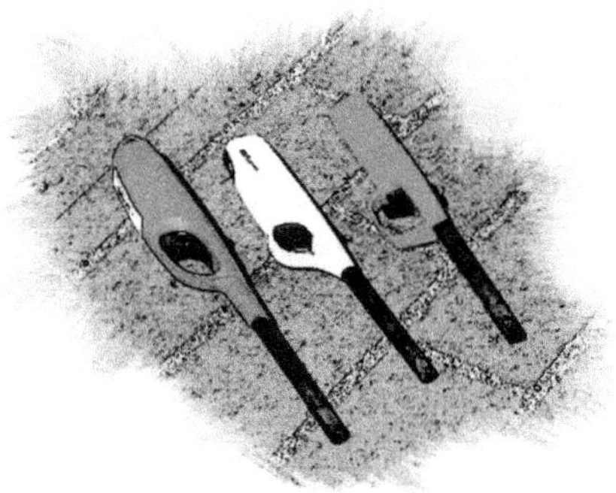

wand lighters

For lump, natural and regular briquette charcoal, invest in a charcoal starter or charcoal chimney, which is basically a large metal can with holes in the bottom and a handle on the side. Line the bottom with crumbled newspaper or tinder, fill it with charcoal and light it from the bottom. The starter will put out a lot of smoke at first.

Or try an electric charcoal starter. Insert the long metal wand into a starter or chimney and fill charcoal loosely around it. Plug in and wait about 10 minutes until charcoal is glowing. But don't forget and leave it for too long or any plastic in the starter handle will melt, which I learned the hard way.

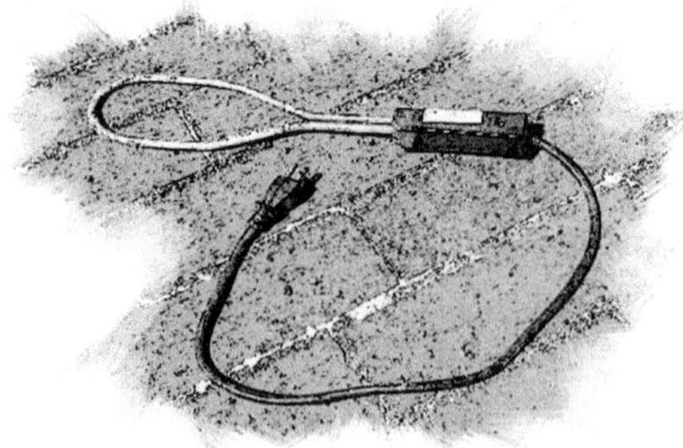

electric charcoal starter

Picnic Eco-Start Charcoal Lighter Gel [www.packserv.com] is an environmentally friendly plant-derived ethanol lighter gel. It's also good for rejuvenating self-lighting charcoal that's gotten old or wet. Look for it in eco and natural food stores.

Another easy technique is to make a smaller fire of self-lighting charcoal. Once flames are present, layer natural charcoal or briquettes loosely on top.

Eco-Start

safety & fire tools

A pair of heat-resistant gloves is handy, especially if your burner does not have handles. You'll also need a yard-long metal rod or poker to stir and adjust the embers, though a long stick will do in a pinch. Hand bellows that pump to dispense a steady stream of air are helpful to encourage recalcitrant charcoal to ignite, but a wide and sturdy fan will also work.

bellows and iron poker

Always have a gallon jug of water on hand to extinguish the coals and put out stray fires. Bring along a fire extinguisher if using your hibachi anywhere near dry grass and other tinder. Don't use the hibachi during drought conditions or when it's windy. Check to see if your county has decreed a ban on open fires due to unsafe conditions.

Fire making is messy. Bring pre-moistened wipes or soapy water and rags for clean up.

fire making skills

When igniting the charcoal directly in the hibachi, make a conical pile. This provides airflow while containing the heat. Once the initial flames have died down, cover the hibachi loosely with the lid (if available) and be sure the vent holes are open.

After igniting the charcoal, wait until there are no flames on the embers. This can take from 10 to 30 minutes, depending on how much and what kind ofcharcoal you're using. Test the heat by tossing on some leaves. They should release smoke, but no flames.

Once the embers have attained this state of heat perfection, spread the charcoal to create a level surface. Smoosh the embers to create lots of hot surface area and an even bed. After several applications of herbs, stir and re-level the embers with metal poker to keep them fresh and hot.

If you've got one handy, turn to a current or former Boy Scout for a lesson in fire tending. These fellas have been trained to make fires in a variety of conditions. Middle-aged barbeque lovers can also be good teachers, as long as they haven't gone soft from using gas units.

extinguishing hot charcoal

The best way to extinguish hot charcoal is to allow the embers to burn up completely so that only ash is left. A tight, non-flammable cover may be put on the hibachi to help extinguish the embers by depriving them of oxygen. But keep in mind that embers can be covered with ash and appear to be out, yet still be flammable. Stir well and check carefully.

If you must leave before the charcoal is burned up, or just want to be sure the embers are out, douse with water. To keep from making a mess of the hibachi, turn the hot charcoal out onto bare dirt and then wet down the embers. Avoid doing this on concrete or pavement because it can leave a gnarly stain.

Ember remains and ash from natural and extrusion charcoal may be scattered or composted. Briquette charcoal ember remains and ash should be disposed of with other garbage.

cautions

Burning charcoal, like burning wood, produces soot particles. Don't breathe the fumes of burning charcoal while it's being ignited, especially if you have respiratory issues. Asthmatics and others with lung ailments should wear a respiratory dust mask.

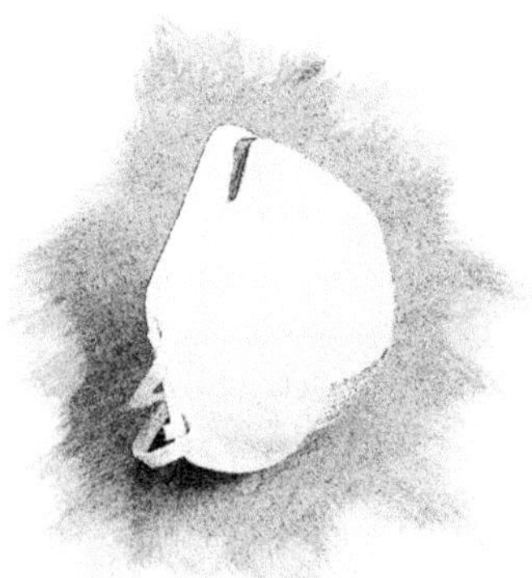

dust mask

Self-lighting charcoal releases volatile organic compounds from the lighter fluid that damage the ozone layer and contribute to air pollution. They are horrid for anyone to breathe.

Be careful around hibachis if you're wearing long or flowing clothes. Human candles can really spoil a gathering. It's always good to keep a small fire extinguisher on hand.

equipment list

Lighting Tools

hibachi, cast-iron stove or fire pit
censer, thurible or chalice
charcoal
charcoal chimney or starter
ethanol lighter fluid
metal poker
bellows or sturdy fan
utility or candle lighter

Safety Tools

heat-resistant gloves
small fire extinguisher or gallon of water
respiratory dust mask
pre-moistened wipes or soapy water
and rags

fire extinguisher

4

burning herbs

smudges ~ offerings ~ element evokers
inhalants ~ immersants

Hibachi Herbal Magic creates industrial-strength purification smudging, dramatic burnt offerings and intense smoke immersions. Your clothes, skin and hair will have a very strong odor afterward. It makes my cats sneeze. Simple airing won't do the trick; it usually takes washing to remove the aroma.

Folks with sensitive skin should moisturize their face and exposed skin for protection before they begin working with smoking herbs. Those with lung issues should consider using a respiratory dust filter mask, remain a good distance from the offerings and not use inhalants or immersants at all.

Keep a small, well-sealed container of fumitory or asafoetida on hand. Sometimes when spiritual energy is raised, not all of it is friendly, causing attendees to get anxious or fearful. If you sense this may be the case, toss fumitory or asafoetida on embers to disperse malevolent energies. For more information, see the Ceremony Safety Herbs section of Moonlady's Magical Herbs.

SECTION MENU

smudges

Instructions: Sprinkle herbs onto hot charcoal and allow the smoke to envelope the entire body. Inhale gently, but do not take the smoke into lungs.

Beltane or Summer Solstice Bonfire

Aroma: herbaceous – slightly sharp and resinous
Ceremonial Use: marking seasonal and social transitions
Significant Days: Beltane, Summer Solstice

Preparation Notes: Blend together.

1/2 cup	elder flower	1 part
1 cup	rosemary	2 parts
1 cup	slippery elm bark	2 parts
1/2 cup	St. John's wort	1 part
1/4 cup	sweet woodruff	1/2 part
1/2 cup	vervain, blue	1 part
1/2 cup	wood betony	1 part

Some fools enjoy leaping through a Beltane or Summer Solstice bonfire. The wiser of us wait until the flames have turned to embers before launching. While there is magic in a fiery leap of faith, we get equal oomph from herbs that facilitate love, divination, and ending quarrels. In this recipe, rosemary salutes the Sun and provides the bulk of the aroma, with blue vervain adding to the purifying power. Slippery elm and wood betony repair quarrels, carrying on the "burying the hatchet" part of Beltane rituals. St. John's Wort brings in the solar focus and adds the love divination so important to Summer Solstice. Sweet woodruff also deepens the solar emphasis.

Feminine Focus

Aroma: resinous – sweetly musky with spicy overtones
Ceremonial Use: purifications; Venus, Moon and women's ceremonies
Significant Days: New and Full Moons; goddess and divine feminine days

Preparation Notes: Crush the cardamom pods, myrrh, sandalwood and valerian root, if necessary, and grind into a rough powder. Add thyme and blue vervain and blend.

1/2 cup	cardamom pod	1 part
1 cup	myrrh resin	2 parts
1/2 cup	sandalwood	1 part
1/4 cup	thyme	1/2 part
1/2 cup	valerian root	1 part
1/2 cup	vervain, blue	1 part

The warm aroma and purifying qualities of the lunar myrrh and sandalwood are paired with the purification punch of blue vervain and thyme. Valerian provides relaxed grounding, while cardamom adds spice and pays tribute to Venus, the goddess of love. (See note about balancing with solar blends in Lunar Purification, below.)

Lunar Purification

Aroma: resinous – sweetly musky with a touch of sharpness
Ceremonial Use: purifications; women's, fertility, Moon and water ceremonies
Significant Days: New and Full Moons; goddess and divine feminine days

Preparation Notes: Crush the calamus, myrrh and sandalwood, if necessary, then grind with the buchu into a rough powder. Add mugwort and wild lettuce and blend.

1/2 cup	buchu	1 part
1/2 cup	calamus root - optional	1 part
1 cup	mugwort	2 parts
1 cup	myrrh resin	2 parts
1 cup	sandalwood	2 parts
1/4 cup	wild lettuce root - optional	1/2 part

This recipe produces a beautiful fluid smoke with a sweet, relaxing aroma. Mugwort, an herb of the Moon, is the core lunar connection. It imparts a bit of a buzz and aids in dream divination. Myrrh and sandalwood provide the base aroma and purifying strength.

The optional calamus and wild lettuce roots contribute spicy notes and are slightly trance inducing, but should not be used with children, teens or anyone on medication for psychiatric conditions. Pregnant and nursing women should avoid mugwort.

Because the herbs in this recipe are linked with the Moon and feminine principles, I recommend following it with a dose of Solar Purification or Masculine Manna smudge, or with a Tree Temple or Sun Salutation offering, for balance.

Masculine Manna

Aroma: spicy – with a touch of sweet
Ceremonial Use: purifications; Mars and Sun ceremonies; warrior and men's ceremonies
Significant Days: New Moons; equinoxes and seasonal dates; god and divine masculine days

Preparation Notes: Crush the allspice, cinnamon, clove, copal, dandelion root and frankincense, if necessary, and then grind into a rough powder. Add hyssop and wood betony and blend. Dust with benzoin resin and blend again.

1/4 cup	allspice	1 part
2 tablespoons	benzoin resin	1/2 part
1/4 cup	cinnamon bark	1 part
2 tablespoons	clove bud	1/2 part
1/4 cup	copal	1 part
1/4 cup	dandelion root	1 part
1/2 cup	frankincense	2 parts
1/4 cup	hyssop	1 part
1/4 cup	wood betony	1 part

This is a spicy smudge with fire and vigor that energizes as much as it purifies and protects. It produces a dense, intense smoke. Consider following it briefly with Feminine Focus or Lunar Purification for balance.

Solar Purification

Aroma: herbaceous – sharp and resinous
Ceremonial Use: purifications; Sun and fire ceremonies; god and divine masculine days
Significant Days: Summer Solstice, New Moons

Preparation Notes: Break up or grind the bay laurel into medium-sized pieces. Add rosemary, white sage and yerba santa and grind to a rough powder. Blend in hyssop. Sprinkle with juniper oil and blend again.

1/2 cup	bay laurel	1 part
1/4 cup	hyssop	1/2 part
15 to 20 drops	juniper oil	15 to 20 drops
1 cup	rosemary	2 parts
2 cups	sage, white	4 parts
1 cup	yerba santa	2 parts

A strong sage smudge can strip your aura clean, but you need a little protection. In this blend, yerba santa provides a protective wrap after hyssop pushes out the negativity and sage takes it away. Bay laurel, rosemary and juniper provide additional purification and protection, and add a green sharpness to the aroma. Be sure to use the *Salvia apina* sold by herb outlets, and not the "sage" found growing wild in the Southwest, which is actually an artemisia. Yerba santa has a strong musty smell, so increase the juniper or rosemary if you prefer.

Because the herbs in this smudge are associated with Sun and masculine principles, they can set things out of balance. I suggest following this smudge with a brief Lunar Purification or Feminine Focus smudge or a Moon Commune offering.

offerings

Instructions: Sprinkle the herbs onto hot charcoal and inhale strongly, but do not take the smoke into lungs. If you wish, allow smoke to envelope entire body as a smudge.

Moon Commune

Aroma: resinous – sweetly musky and warm
Ceremonial Use: purifications; women's, fertility, Moon and water ceremonies
Significant Days: New and Full Moons

Preparation Notes: Crush the myrrh and sandalwood, if necessary, and then grind with the buchu into a rough powder. Add mugwort and wild lettuce and blend.

1/4 cup	buchu - optional	1/2 part
1/2 cup	mugwort	1 part
1 cup	myrrh resin	2 parts
1 cup	sandalwood	2 parts
1/2 cup	wild lettuce root - optional	1 part

Burn these lunar herbs as an offering to the Moon. They impart a rich, warm, mutilayered aroma with a strong emotional impact. Based on mugwort, herb of the Moon, myrrh and sandalwood, which add the aromatic tone along with strong qualities of purification and protection. If children, teens or anyone on medication for psychiatric illness are not present, you can deepen the impact by including buchu and wild lettuce to expand the mind. Pregnant and nursing women should avoid mugwort.

Passages

Aroma: resinous – with much spice and sharpness
Ceremonial Use: cremations; funerals and memorial services
Significant Days: Day of the Dead, Divali, Samhain

Preparation Notes: Crush the copal, elder wood, mandrake root, myrrh, poplar bud and sandalwood, if necessary, and then grind into a rough and very sticky powder. Add anise seed, basil, Dittany of Crete and rosemary and blend. Sprinkle with cypress oil and blend again.

2 tablespoons	anise seed	1/2 part
1/4 cup	basil	1 part
1 cup	copal resin	4 parts
10 to 20 drops	cypress oil	10 to 20 drops
1/4 cup	Dittany of Crete	1 part
1/4 cup	elder wood	1 part
2 tablespoons	mandrake root	1/2 part
1 cup	myrrh resin	4 parts
1/2 cup	poplar bud	2 parts
1/4 cup	rosemary	1 part
1/2 cup	sandalwood	2 parts

For use at the end of life, this recipe features herbs that honor the deceased and assist their passages, either from the physical body or between worlds. Use this blend to dress the body before burial or cremation, or for herbs to toss into the grave. Burn the blend at memorial services, funerals and ancestor observances.

Releasing

Aroma: resinous – spicy and musky with a hint of sweetness
Ceremonial Use: burning bowl services; habit breaking; separations and divorces
Significant Days: 4th lunar quarter, New Year

Preparation Notes: Crush the clove, coriander, galangal root, myrrh and slippery elm if necessary, and grind into a rough powder. Add hyssop, rosemary and wood betony and blend. Dust with benzoin and blend again.

2 tablespoons	benzoin resin	1/2 part
1/4 cup	clove bud	1 part
1/4 cup	coriander	1 part
1/4 cup	galangal root	1 part
1/4 cup	hyssop	1 part
1/2 cup	myrrh resin	2 parts
1/4 cup	rosemary	1 part
1/2 cup	slippery elm bark	2 parts
1/4 cup	wood betony	1 part

It can be hard to let go. Burning this herbal blend gives focus to our intentions for change. Burn these herbs with slips of paper listing who or what is to be released. This blend facilitates the separation of unhealthy relationships and helps end gossip and malingering. It's also helpful for breaking any kind of pattern. I have had some howling good ceremonies around the hibachi with this one as women shouted out their released burdens and danced. This blend works well as a smudge.

Spirit Food

Aroma: resinous – sweet with a slight sharp note
Ceremonial Use: ancestor remembrances; funerals and memorial services; evocations and honorings of spirits and spirit guides
Significant Days: Day of the Dead, Samhain, Divali

Preparation Notes: Crush the copal, myrrh and poplar bud, if necessary, and grind into a rough and very sticky powder. Add Dittany of Crete and blend.

1 cup	copal resin	2 parts
1/4 cup	Dittany of Crete	1/2 part
1/4 cup	myrrh resin	1/2 part
1/2 cup	poplar bud (Balm of Gilead)	1 part

Burn these herbs to nourish the spirit world. Copal is an integral part of Day of the Dead ceremonies in Mexico. Poplar buds (Balm of Gilead) assists in releasing the spirits from their domain and Dittany of Crete helps them to manifest in ours. The lush smoke beckons to spiritual entities and sustains a connection from beyond the veil.

Sun Salutation

Aroma: resinous – with vanilla, spice and a touch of sharpness
Ceremonial Use: men's ceremonies; Sun and fire ceremonies; god and divine masculine days
Significant Days: Solstices, Equinoxes

Preparation Notes: Crush the angelica root, cinnamon, copal and frankincense, if necessary, and grind into a rough powder. Add St. John's wort and blend. Lightly dust with acacia (gum arabic) and benzoin and blend again.

2 tablespoons	acacia (gum arabic)	1/4 part
1/4 cup	angelica root	1/2 part
2 tablespoons	benzoin resin	1/4 part
1/4 cup	chamomile	1/2 part
1/2 cup	cinnamon bark	1 part
1 cup	copal resin	2 parts
1 cup	frankincense resin	2 parts
1/2 cup	St. John's wort	1 part

A medley of solar herbs with high spiritual vibrations. Frankincense, the most fiery of all the resins, serves as the aromatic base, with copal adding a bit of mellow sweetness. Angelica and St. John's wort impart visionary and divination qualities, with acacia (gum arabic) and benzoin contributing warm undertones. Cinnamon bark adds fire and spice.

Tree Temple

Aroma: resinous – sweetly sharp with vanilla and spice
Ceremonial Use: all sacred gatherings, World Tree
Significant Days: Yule

Preparation Notes: Crush the copal, dragon's blood, frankincense, myrrh and sandalwood, if necessary, and grind into a rough powder. Sprinkle the cypress oil on top and blend. Lightly dust with acacia (gum arabic) and benzoin powders and blend.

2 tablespoons	acacia (gum arabic)	1/4 part
2 tablespoons	benzoin resin	1/4 part
1/2 cup	copal resin	1 part
10 to 15 drops	cypress oil	10 to 15 drops
2 tablespoons	dragon's blood resin	1/4 part
1/2 cup	frankincense resin	1 part
1/2 cup	myrrh resin	1 part
1/2 cup	sandalwood	1 part

This is a great all-around aromatic temple blend that enhances any sacred setting or occasion, a perfect medley of mind, spirit and emotion, Sun and Moon, and all four elements. Breathing this aroma is to take communion with the World Tree and merge with our history as human beings.

element evokers

Instructions: Sprinkle the herbs onto hot charcoal and inhale gently, but do not take the smoke deep into lungs. If you wish, allow smoke to envelope entire body as a smudge.

Air

Aroma: spicy – with warm undertones
Ceremonial Use: evoking the direction of east and the power of air and its attributes: intellect, ideas, invention
Significant Days: New and Full Moons in air signs, air deity days

Preparation Notes: Lightly grind hops, blend with anise and caraway. Dust with acacia (gum arabic) and benzoin, and blend again.

1/4 cup	anise seed	1/2 part
2 tablespoons	acacia (gum arabic)	1/4 part
2 tablespoons	benzoin resin	1/4 part
1/4 cup	caraway seed	1/2 part
1/2 cup	hops	1 part

Earth

Aroma: earthy – with a sharp edge
Ceremonial Use: evoking the direction of north and the power of earth and its attributes: stability, sustenance, wisdom

Significant Days: New and Full Moons in earth signs, earth deity days

Preparation Notes: Crush the vetivert root, if necessary, and grind into a rough powder. Blend with patchouli and blue vervain. Sprinkle with cypress oil and blend again.

5 to 10 drops	cypress oil	5 to 10 drops
1 cup	patchouli	2 parts
5 to 10 drops	vetivert root	5 to 10 drops
1/2 cup	vervain, blue	1 part

Fire

Aroma: spicy – with a highlights of sharp and sweet
Ceremonial Use: evoking the direction of south and the power of fire and its attributes: spirit, passion, creativity
Significant Days: Summer and Winter Solstices, New and Full Moons in fire signs, fire deity days

Preparation Notes: Crush the allspice, angelica root, coriander, dragon's blood, frankincense and galangal root, if necessary, and grind into a rough powder. Add hyssop and blend.

1/4 cup	allspice	1 part
1/4 cup	angelica root	1 part
1/4 cup	coriander	1 part
1 tablespoon	dragon's blood resin	1/4 part
1/4 cup	frankincense resin	1 part
1/4 cup	galangal root	1 part
1/4 cup	hyssop	1 part

Water

Aroma: earthy – with hints of sharp and spice
Ceremonial Use: evoking the direction of west and the power of water and its attributes: emotion, communication, subconscious
Significant Days: New and Full Moons in water signs, water deity days

Preparation Notes: Crush the poplar bud, cardamom pod, myrrh, calamus root and valerian root, if necessary, and grind into a rough powder. Lightly grind the coltsfoot and blend with the other ingredients.

1/4 cup	calamus root	1 part
1/4 cup	cardamom pod	1 part
1/2 cup	coltsfoot	2 parts
1/2 cup	myrrh resin	2 parts
1/4 cup	poplar bud (Balm of Gilead)	1 part
1/4 cup	valerian root	1 part

inhalants

Instructions: Using an inhalant is similar to making an offering, but is not done for spiritual effect. Sprinkle the herbs onto hot charcoal and inhale strongly, being careful not take too deep into lungs. Be sure to stand far enough back so that the smoke is cool. If you wish, allow smoke to envelope entire body as a smudge.

Chill Out

Aroma: resinous – warm & musky
Ceremonial Use: to mellow out

Preparation Notes: Crush the myrrh and valerian root, if necessary, and grind into a rough powder. Blend with mugwort.

1/2 cup	mugwort	1 part
1/2 cup	myrrh resin	1 part
1/2 cup	valerian root	1 part

When the party around the bonfire just won't end, yet most attendees are ready for sleep, toss some of this blend on the embers. It's also useful for calming overly aroused or agitated people.

Mind Sharpen

Aroma: herbaceous – with a resinous edge
Ceremonial Use: to sharpen focus or sober up

Preparation Notes: Crush the frankincense, if necessary, and grind into a rough powder. Lightly grind the bay laurel and rosemary and blend with frankincense. Dust with benzoin and blend. Sprinkle with camphor oil and blend again.

1/2 cup	bay laurel	1 part
2 tablespoons	benzoin resin	1/4 part
15 to 20 drops	camphor oil	15 to 20 drops
1/2 cup	frankincense resin	1 part
1/2 cup	rosemary	1 part

Burn this blend at those times when a bit too much fun has been had with intoxicants and sexual proclivities. It can bring about a clarity that's helpful with divination or in other situations when an alert mind is needed. It also aids in waking up sleepy people or keeping them awake.

immersants

Instructions: Sprinkle the herbs onto hot charcoal and allow the smoke to envelope entire body. Inhale strongly, taking the smoke deep into lungs.

Immersants are like smudges, but with an emphasis on mental and spiritual expansion. While they are supposed to be breathed in, do not inhale hot smoke. Stand far enough back so that it's cool and do not use inhalants without Lung Buffer blend. Active substances can also be absorbed through the skin if immersing is done naked or lightly clothed.

These blends are to be used only by adults in a private setting. Partake gradually and at a slow pace so that you can judge your dose. These blends are not for use by children or teens. They are not appropriate for anyone on psychiatric medication or for pregnant or nursing women. Do not drive or operate machinery on these blends.

Lung Buffer

Aroma: herbaceous – warm and spicy

Preparation Notes: Crush the pleurisy root, if necessary, and grind finely. Add the remaining herbs, which will be fluffy and somewhat difficult to mix.

1/2 cup	coltsfoot	1 part
1/2 cup	horehound and/or great mullein	1 part
1/4 cup	lungwort	1/2 part
1/8 cup	pleurisy root	1/4 part

This recipe is based on moist herbs high in mucilage that are known to sooth the lungs when inhaled as smoke. Coltsfoot has an extremely attractive aroma and is integral to non-tobacco smoking blends.

Aphrodite's Desire

Aroma: herbaceous – warm and spicy
Ceremonial Use: women's and fertility ceremonies
Significant Days: Beltane

Preparation Notes: Crush the cardamom pods, coriander seed, mandrake root, muira pauma and vetivert root, if necessary, and grind into a rough powder. Be sure the mandrake and muira pauma are ground up well. Add anise seed, damiana, patchouli, yerba mate and Lung Buffer and blend. Sprinkle with clary sage oil and blend again.

2 tablespoons	anise seed	1/4 part
1/2 cup	cardamom pod	1 part
1/4 cup	coriander seed	1/2 part
1 cup	damiana	2 parts
1 tablespoon	mandrake root	1/8 part
1/2 cup	muira pauma	1 part
1/2 cup	patchouli	1 part
15 to 20 drops	sage, clary oil	15 to 20 drops
15 to 20 drops	vetivert root	15 to 20 drops
1/2 cup	yerba mate	1 part
1/4 cup	Lung Buffer	1/2 part

This is a blend of aphrodisiac herbs with an emphasis on the female libido. The spicy cardamon and musky patchouli make a luscious aroma base that supports the leafy spiciness of damiana and yerba mate. The deep aroma masks the harsh but effective muira pauma and mandrake. Be careful with this blend; it really is potent.

Deep Meditation

Aroma: herbaceous – sweet musk
Ceremonial Use: spiritual communions; trances; meditation
Significant Days: Full Moons; Wesak

Preparation Notes: Crush the mandrake root and myrrh, if necessary, and grind into a rough powder. Add anise seed, mugwort, scullcap (skullcap), blue vervain and wild lettuce, plus Lung Buffer, and blend.

2 tablespoons	anise seed	1/4 part
2 tablespoons	mandrake root	1/4 part
1/2 cup	mugwort	1 part
1/4 cup	myrrh resin	1/2 part
1/2 cup	scullcap	1 part
2 tablespoons	vervain, blue	1/4 part
1/2 cup	wild lettuce root	1 part
1/4 cup	Lung Buffer Blend	1/2 part

This blend leads the inhaler into deep alpha and theta states, and assists with vivid dreaming. The scullcap makes it very soothing to the nerves. Myrrh and mugwort open the emotions to the mind-expanding effects of wild lettuce and mandrake. Use this blend sparingly.

Divination & Dream Enhance

Aroma: herbaceous – sweet musk and spice
Ceremonial Use: dream divination
Significant Days: Full Moons; Summer Solstice

Preparation Notes: Crush the galangal root, if necessary, then grind with the buchu into a rough powder. Add St. John's wort, wild lettuce and wood betony, plus Lung Buffer, and blend.

1/4 cup	buchu	1/2 part
1/2 cup	galangal root	1 part
1/2 cup	mugwort	1 part
1/4 cup	St. John's wort	1/2 part
1/4 cup	wild lettuce root	1/2 part
1/2 cup	wood betony	1 part
1/4 cup	Lung Buffer	1/2 part

This blend helps us enter deep alpha and theta states with herbs that inspire vivid and sometimes prophetic dreaming. Use this blend sparingly.

Trance

Aroma: earthy – peppery ginger with musky undertones
Ceremonial Use: spiritual communion; trances; drumming
Significant Days: Full Moons

Preparation Notes: Crush the angelica, calamus, dandelion and galangal roots and kava kava, if necessary, into a rough powder. Add anise, damiana, mugwort and Lung Buffer, and blend. Sprinkle with clary sage oil and blend again.

1 cup	angelica root	2 parts
2 tablespoons	anise seed	1/4 part
1/2 cup	calamus root	1 part
1/2 cup	damiana	1 part
1/2 cup	dandelion root	1 part
1 cup	galangal root	2 parts
1 cup	kava kava	2 parts
1 cup	mugwort	2 parts
15 to 20 drops	sage, clary oil	15 to 20 drops
1 cup	Lung Buffer	2 parts

Here we have the hit parade of psychotropic roots, plus some trippy leaves and woods. Burn these herbs on very hot charcoal. They are all somewhat psychedelic, hallucinatory and visionary with a lustful edge. The smoke can be somewhat harsh; if so, increase the Lung Buffer.

strewing herbs

positive protected space ~ sacred feet ~ happy people

Strewing is a lost art. Formerly a mainstay of temple life, it's a celebration of herbs in all their untouched glory. They're powerful enough to shift energy by their presence alone. There is a gentle agricultural evocation in the motion of spreading herbs evenly across the ground. The act of walking upon them, seemingly so disrespectful, is what releases their power.

To prepare a public park for a spiritual ceremony, I'll strew herbs in waves, starting with the Positive Space blend in a clockwise, energy-dispersing motion to cancel out negative energy that may be present. After giving it a few minutes to work, I layer Prayer Dance counter-clockwise over it. This blend amplifies a site's sacred energies. Completing the site preparation, I clockwise strew Perimeter Protection around the outside of the ceremonial space.

Indoors, I strew Positive Space clockwise and perform a thorough smudging. While the strewn herbs and smoke simmer, I clockwise toss Perimeter Protection around the outside of the house or structure. Then I vacuum or sweep up inside, open doors and turn on fans to move the smoke out. Bowls of Happy Mix, Prosperity Potpourri and Mellow Yellow, plus significant candles, complete the ceremony.

SECTION MENU

ceremonies & sacred space

Instructions: Strew the herbs lightly but thoroughly with sacred intent. If used indoors, vacuum afterwards as the seeds are very attractive to bugs and rodents.

Perimeter Protection

Aroma: herbaceous
Ceremonial Use: prayer dance and meditation spaces; altar areas; spaces used for ceremonial gatherings; sacred sites

Preparation Notes: Just mix and strew.

I cup	vervain, blue	I part
I cup	wood betony	I part

Blue vervain deflects negative energy and wood betony creates a strongly protective, enveloping boundary. Use this blend to define the perimeter of a ceremony space. Strew it double-strength across doorways, entrances and walkways. As a test, I've laid this across a jogging path and watched people – and dogs! – jump over it.

Perimeter Protection blend is great strewn around the outside of your abode or other site. Strew in a clockwise motion that moves energy outward. When I give talks in public buildings, I'll strew a small discrete line across the doorway of my room to keep negativity out. It's helpful in office doorways, too.

For house blessings, I clockwise strew Perimeter Protection around the outside of the yard or open area, and once again around the base of the house, with double lines across windowsills and doorways.

Positive Space

Aroma: spicy – sharp with a wisp of apple & licorice
Ceremonial Use: sacred space and general site preparation, house and site blessings

Preparation Notes: Grind the calamus root into a fine powder and blend with the remaining ingredients. If you grind the chamomile flowers first, or break them up by hand, you'll get more strewing for your money, but it won't look as nice.

I/2 cup	anise seed	I part
I/2 cup	caraway seed	I part
I/4 cup	calamus root	I/2 part
I cup	chamomile	2 parts
I/2 cup	fennel seed	I part
I cup	hyssop	2 parts
I/2 cup	vervain, blue	I part

This blend is based on sweet, happy, little chamomile, the Pollyanna herb that's super strong at counteracting negativity, plus its butch purifying pal, blue vervain. Also included is hyssop, which flat out frightens negativity away. The carminative seeds anise, caraway and fennel absorb any negative charge. Calamus brings in a bright energy. Sprinkle this blend lightly in areas where people gather. Give it a few minutes to work before letting people in.

Be careful with this blend in areas where the seeds might mature into plants and disrupt an eco-system. This may not be a problem in parks and other areas that get mowed regularly. If sprouting is an issue, bake the seeds first in a 400-degree oven for five minutes.

Prayer Feet

Aroma: herbaceous – new-mown hay with a whiff of apple
Ceremonial Use: prayer dance and meditation spaces; altar areas; spaces used for ceremonial gatherings; sacred sites

Preparation Notes: Work the corn silk into the corn meal with your fingers. If you very lightly grind the chamomile and hops flowers first, or break them up by hand, you'll get more strewing for your money, but it won't look as nice. Then mix the remaining ingredients and strew.

1 cup	chamomile	1 part
2 cups	corn meal	2 parts
1 cup	corn silk	1 part
1 cup	dandelion leaf	1 part
2 cups	hops	2 parts
1 cup	pennyroyal	1 part

These herbs are a beautiful, nurturing offering to the Earth and a terrific aid to help the feet connect with Earth energies. People love dancing on this blend! It's good for the feet and the Earth.

Strew this blend where people will be gathering in ceremony, with extra amounts at entrances, the center and wherever the event principals will be standing. Strew where you sit in meditation or do yoga. Strew along pilgrimage paths and at wedding chancels. This recipe is perfect for prayer dancing and amazingly powerful for communing at outdoor sacred sites.

indoor & confined space

Instructions: Use these potpourris in containers indoors or in confined spaces like porches, awnings and tents. The recipes have been developed to be attractive and aromatic, while also being very effective. People are compelled to run their fingers through these mixes, which activates them and releases the aroma.

Happy Mix

Aroma: spicy – with a touch of heat and sweet
Ceremonial Use: happiness blessings; positive space

Preparation Notes: Just mix and fill containers.

1/4 cup	anise seed	1 part
1/4 cup	caraway seed	1 part
1/4 cup	cardamom seed	1 part
1/4 cup	clove bud	1 part
1/4 cup	coriander	1 part
1/4 cup	dill seed	1 part
1/4 cup	fennel seed	1 part
1/2 cup	peppercorn	2 parts
1/2 cup	salt	2 parts

Based on the carminative anise, caraway, dill and fennel seeds that absorb negativity. Cardamom and clove sweeten the smell, and coriander promotes pleasantness. Peppercorns and salt are powerful negativity adjusters. Use chunky crystal salt made from evaporated seawater. Because this blend contains salt, it can not be used for strewing outdoors.

Set out Happy Mix in small bowls or ornate containers. With its mix of seed shapes and colors contrasting with white salt and black peppercorns, it's very attractive. You can also use different colors of salt and pepper.

One woman I know kept a small bowl on her desktop at work and would run her fingers though it whenever her cranky boss came into the room. Then he noticed her habit and started doing it, too. Their talks go better now.

Mellow Yellow

Aroma: herbaceous – with a wisp of apple and floral highlights
Ceremonial Use: positive space

Preparation Notes: Blend together.

1/4 cup	calendula	1 part
1/2 cup	chamomile	2 parts
1/4 cup	elder flower	1 part
1/4 cup	hops	1 part
1/2 cup	lavender	2 parts

This blend is based on flowers, yet it's not floral. Hops, chamomile and calendula all have a pleasant piquant aromas, a bit like new mown hay, that men enjoy. Elder flowers provide a warm undertone and lavender brightens the aroma. Keep it next to your bed and fondle to release the aroma before sleep.

Prosperity Potpourri

Aroma: spicy – and sweet
Ceremonial Use: prosperity blessings; positive space

Preparation Notes: Break the cinnamon bark into medium pieces. Blend with remaining ingredients.

1/4 cup	allspice	1 part
1/4 cup	cardamom pod	1 part
1/4 cup	cinnamon bark	1 part
1/4 cup	clove bud	1 part
1/4 cup	juniper berry	1 part
1/4 cup	poplar bud (Balm of Gilead)	1 part

This is terrific paired with donation containers or at raffle or silent auction tables. Place bowls of this blend near cashiers and at any location where money changes hands. It's great for home offices, studios and other places of business and commerce.

6

moonlady's magical herbs

herbal info ~ lung herbs ~ ceremony safety herbs ~ salt

Herbs hold such promise. Unlike the ephemeral flower that fades, most herbs retain their potency even when dry. Integral to the landscape, yet rarely overbearing, herbs remain a pleasant surprise.

Over time, however, the love affair can fray. It's tough on herbs to live up to folklore's enthusiastic claims. Below are ceremonial herbs that I remain blissfully in love with, even after all these years.

Concluding this chapter is a list of lung-friendly herbs for use in blends that are inhaled. Next are herbs that dispel malevolent energies and subdue overly intoxicated or emotional people. A short treatise on salt rounds things out.

These descriptions are highly personal and not intended to be complete. Many excellent herb books and web sites with detailed information exist; one of them will be perfect for your needs. A few of my favorites are listed in Resources.

SECTION MENU

ceremonial herbs

acacia (gum arabic)

Botanical Name: *Acacia nilotica*
Part of Plant: sap
Aroma: sweet – faintly vanilla
Planetary Ruler: Sun
Element: air
Sexuality: masculine
Blends: **Offering:** Sun Salutation, Tree Temple. **Element:** air.

Qualities: The sap from a spiny shrub or small tree that grows in sandy dry areas is dried and ground to a fine white powder. Some acacias, like those featured in Egyptian myths of immortality, are considered sacred. Gum Arabic adds a very light undertone for blending disparate ingredients in incense. Mix with powders when you want them to cling to something, such as when adding benzoin or dragon's blood powder to resins.

allspice

Botanical Name: *Pimento dioica*
Part of Plant: berry
Aroma: spicy – a blend of cinnamon and nutmeg
Planetary Ruler: Mars
Element: fire
Sexuality: masculine
Blends: **Smudge:** Masculine Manna. **Element:** fire. **Potpourri:** Prosperity.

Qualities: A large berry for a spice, it evokes prosperity.

angelica

Botanical Name: *Angelica archangelica*
Part of Plant: root
Aroma: earthy – slight spice
Planetary Ruler: Sun
Element: fire
Sexuality: masculine
Blends: **Offering:** Sun Salutation. **Element:** fire.
Immersant: Trance.

Qualities: A beautiful tall plant with lacy leaves and delicate flowers, the genteel topside belies the root's psychotropic punch. The name refers to the angelic visions it promotes. Medieval Europe's most popular trippy root. Use only occasionally.

angelica

anise

Botanical Name: *Pimpinella anisum*
Part of Plant: seed
Aroma: sharp – anise, licorice

Planetary Ruler: Moon
Element: air
Sexuality: masculine
Blends: **Offering:** Passages. **Element:** air. **Immersant:** Aphrodite's Desire, Deep Meditation, Trance. **Strew:** Positive Space. **Potpourri:** Happy Mix.

Qualities: Anise is one of the carminative plants – anise, cumin, dill and fennel – all of which have large umbrella-shaped flower clusters whose seeds absorb gas and generally make the gut feel good. Logic goes that if these seeds absorb the negative inside us, they can do the same outside of us, providing protection on many levels. Anise is an especially happy and versatile plant. Some folks find it makes them frisky, while it provokes visions in others.

basil

Botanical Name: *Ocymum basilium*
Part of Plant: leaf
Aroma: herbaceous – sharp with strong licorice tone
Planetary Ruler: Mars
Element: fire
Sexuality: masculine
Blends: **Offering:** Passages.

basil

Qualities: This favorite seasoning of Italian cooking has a much longer history as a sacred herb, especially in India. Basil is held as a plant of passage though death or initiations where submission is key. There are many different kinds of basil. Use holy basil (Ocymum tenuiflorum or sanctum) when you can find it, often found with Indian cooking supplies as tulasi.

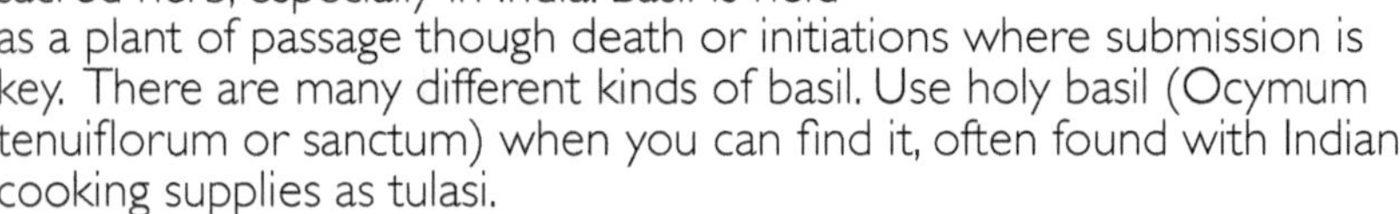

bay laurel

Botanical Name: *Laurus nobilis*
Part of Plant: leaf
Aroma: herbaceous – sharp with a pepper edge
Planetary Ruler: Sun
Element: fire
Sexuality: masculine
Blends: **Smudge:** Solar Purification. **Inhalant:** Mind Sharpen.

bay laurel

Qualities: An herb of honor, prophecy and wisdom, bay laurel clears the mind and enhances stability.

benzoin

Botanical Name: *Styrax benzoin*
Part of Plant: bark resin
Aroma: basalmic – sweet and vanilla-ish

Planetary Ruler: Mars
Element: air
Sexuality: masculine
Blends: **Smudge:** Masculine Manna. **Offering:** Releasing, Sun Salutation, Tree Temple. **Element:** air. **Inhalant:** Mind Sharpen.

Qualities: The white balsamic resin from the bark of a variety of Styrax trees clears out old energies and energizes the physical body. It also purifies and focuses the mind. The warm and soothing aroma helps blend multiple aromas.

buchu

Botanical Name: *Barosma betulina*
Part of Plant: leaf, stem
Aroma: herbaceous – bitter, similar to rue with a woodsy edge
Planetary Ruler: Moon
Element: water
Sexuality: feminine
Blends: **Smudge:** Lunar Purification. **Offering:** Moon Commune. **Immersant:** Divination & Dream Enhance.

Qualities: A wildly psychotropic and lunar plant, buchu enhances psychic abilities, stimulates prophetic dreams and imparts a touch of the werewolf. (Just kidding about that last one.) This potent plant bears a feminine emotional punch. The smoke is very harsh, but the fresh leaves make a piquant flavoring for brandy and tonics.

calamus

Botanical Name: *Acorus calamus*
Part of Plant: root
Aroma: earthy – musky with ginger tones
Planetary Ruler: Moon (Drew)
Element: water
Sexuality: feminine
Blends: **Smudge:** Lunar Purification. **Element:** water. **Immersant:** Trance. **Strew:** Positive Space.

Qualities: Also known as sweet flag or sweet sedge, this vigorous aquatic plant is a mild psychedelic with a peppy lift. Many a besotted wanderer has been found waist-deep in marshes chewing this root, which grows worldwide. It inspired some of Walt Whitman's wackier ballads.

calendula (marigold)

Botanical Name: *Calendula officinalis*
Part of Plant: flower petal
Aroma: floral – sharp, a bit acrid
Planetary Ruler: Sun

calendula

Element: fire
Sexuality: masculine
Blends: **Strew:** Mellow Yellow.

Qualities: Promotes well being and energizes. Sacred to many Mesoamerican goddesses.

camphor

Botanical Name: *Cinnamonum camphora*
Part of Plant: resin
Aroma: resinous – sharp, eucalyptus-like
Planetary Ruler: Moon
Element: water
Sexuality: feminine
Blends: **Inhalant:** Mind Sharpen.

Qualities: The aroma of camphor can help bring focus to someone who's overly emotional or libidinous, disassociating, spacing out, or otherwise going over the edge. It's sort of like psychological smelling salts. The essential oil from *Cinnamonum camphora* is more common than bulk camphor, which comes as beige granules. Apply oil to a cotton ball and pass it beneath the nose. Or saturate organic matter with oil, place it on embers and inhale the aroma. Avoid the small camphor tablets used in Hindu temple and wedding poojas, and the camphor found in drugstores. These are made of synthetic camphor that is very nasty, worse than the toxic chemicals in mothballs.

caraway

Botanical Name: *Carum carvi*
Part of Plant: seed
Aroma: sharp – pungent, anise-like
Planetary Ruler: Mercury
Element: air
Sexuality: masculine
Blends: **Element:** air. **Strew:** Positive Space. **Potpourri:** Happy Mix.

Qualities: One of the carminatives, caraway contains a lot of aroma and negativity-absorbing power.

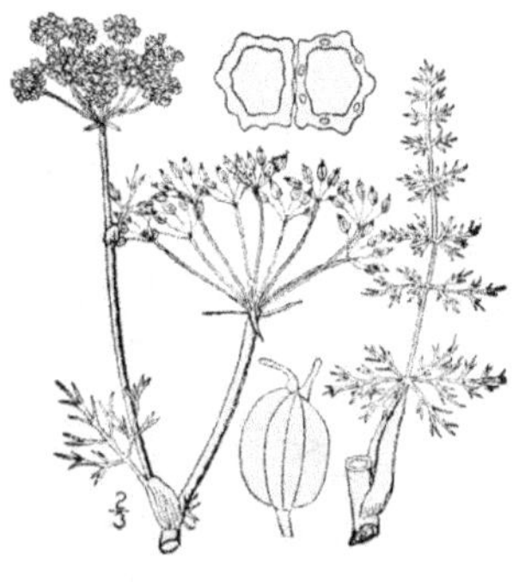
caraway

cardamom

Botanical Name: *Elettaria cardamomum*
Part of Plant: seed pod, seed
Aroma: spicy – sweet and a bit pungent
Planetary Ruler: Venus
Element: water
Sexuality: feminine
Blends: **Smudge:** Feminine Focus. **Element:** water. **Immersant:**

Aphrodite's Desire. **Potpourri:** Happy Mix, Prosperity Potpourri.

Qualities: The aroma of cardamom inspires not lust but love in men and women. Makes everything mellow. For an aphrodisiac effect, toss some seeds or pods in your hot chocolate, coffee or tea. The pod is best for burning and potpourri. Use the seed for strewing.

chamomile, common

Botanical Name: *Anthemis nobilis*
Part of Plant: flower
Aroma: floral – blend of light apple and clover
Planetary Ruler: Sun
Element: water
Sexuality: feminine
Blends: **Offering:** Sun Salutation. **Strew:** Positive Space, Prayer Feet. **Potpourri:** Mellow Yellow.

chamomile

Qualities: Chamomile is like the charming, refined Southern woman who can hog-tie you in ten-seconds flat. It's a sweet, small yellow flower that smells like a meadow, yet nothing's its equal for counteracting the previous negative charge of a space. Walked upon it's very relaxing to the feet.

cinnamon

Botanical Name: *Cinnamomum zeylanicum*
Part of Plant: bark
Aroma: spicy – warm, sweet, slightly sharp
Planetary Ruler: Mercury
Element: fire
Sexuality: masculine
Blends: **Smudge:** Masculine Manna. **Offering:** Sun Salutation. **Potpourri:** Prosperity.

Qualities: A culinary plant with a magical pedigree, cinnamon boasts a fiery taste and provides an avenue to spirit and higher consciousness.

clove

Botanical Name: *Syzygium Icimaticum*
Part of Plant: bud
Aroma: spicy – hot, sharp
Planetary Ruler: Uranus
Element: fire
Sexuality: masculine
Blends: **Smudge:** Masculine Manna. **Offering:** Releasing. **Potpourri:** Happy Mix, Prosperity

Qualities: This is the spiciest of the spices and fiery as well. Clove pierces the mind, enabling memories to arise, imprint or release. Like many spices, it's also associated with prosperity.

coltsfoot

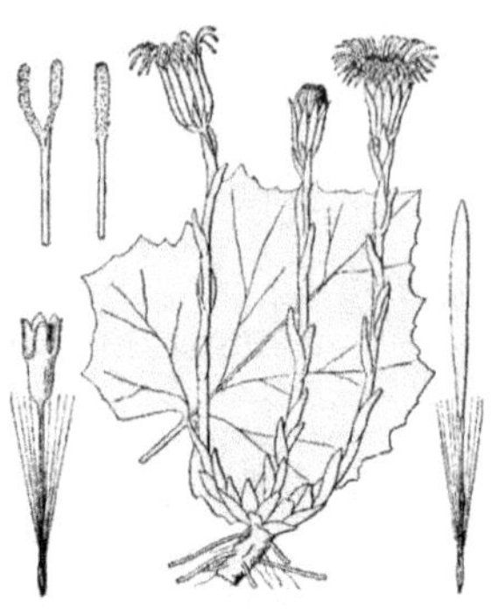

coltsfoot

Botanical Name: *Tussilago farfara*
Part of Plant: leaf
Aroma: herbaceous – warm, vanilla, mildly spicy
Planetary Ruler: Venus
Element: water
Sexuality: feminine
Blends: **Offering:** water. **Immersant:** Lung Buffer.

Qualities: When used as a tea, candy or smoke, coltsfoot can counter coughs and encourage tranquility.

copal

Botanical Name: *Bursera odorata* (Drew), but also other diverse plant sources
Part of Plant: resin
Aroma: sweet – warm and resinous with a slight spicy fruitiness
Planetary Ruler: Sun
Element: fire
Sexuality: masculine
Blends: **Smudge:** Masculine Manna. **Offering:** Passages, Spirit Food, Sun Salutation, Tree Temple.

Qualities: While trees that produce copal are grown worldwide, the resin is most popular in Mesoamerica, Central and South America and serves as a New World frankincense. The pale yellow resin is burned in ceremonies as food for deities. Though it is masculine in nature, its aroma can stimulate strong emotions.

coriander

Botanical Name: *Coriandrum sativum*
Part of Plant: seed
Aroma: sharp – licorice-like with a green edge
Planetary Ruler: Mars, Moon
Element: fire
Sexuality: masculine
Blends: **Offering:** Releasing. **Element:** Fire. **Immersant:** Aphrodite's Desire. **Potpourri:** Happy Mix.

coriander

Qualities: Coriander promotes pleasantness in all unions.

corn

Botanical Name: *Zea mays*

Part of Plant: kernel, silk
Aroma: cereal – mild
Planetary Ruler: Venus (Drew)
Element: earth
Sexuality: feminine
Blends: **Strew:** Prayer Feet.

corn

Qualities: Corn Mother's gift to North America remains the culinary staple of many cultures. It is the offering that best captures the New World's continental Earth spirit. Strewing with the various colors of cornmeal – including yellow, red and blue – can be an art form. Buy organic corn meal, of course. Use a heavier application to outline sacred areas such as altars, however, for that you might consider inexpensive horticultural cornmeal available at nurseries (which won't be organic). Corn silk represents the maiden and fertility aspects of corn. It comes in a wild tangle of fibers that are a challenge to blend.

cypress

Botanical Name: *Cupressus sempervirens*
Part of Plant: wood
Aroma: resinous – evergreen a bit woody
Planetary Ruler: Saturn, Neptune
Element: earth
Sexuality: feminine
Blends: **Offering:** Passages, Tree Temple. **Element:** earth.

Qualities: The evergreen Mediterranean cypress has been a sacred symbol of immortality, from ancient Egyptian coffins to the Christian cross. It's a long lived tree that is resistant to decay and fire. Unlike most evergreens, it possesses a feminine earth energy, rather than fire or air. Cupressus is the most widely distributed conifer family, so local varieties abound. For the blends in this book stick with Mediterranean cypress, which is commonly available as an essential oil.

damiana

Botanical Name: *Turnera aphrodisiaca*
Part of Plant: leaf
Aroma: herbaceous – sweet, musky
Planetary Ruler: Pluto
Element: fire
Sexuality: masculine
Blends: **Immersant:** Aphrodite's Desire, Trance.

Qualities: With a plant named damiana, you know it's a little devilish, or at least naughty. Indeed, this Mexican herb is known to inspire lust in women and visions in both sexes. Look for damiana liqueur sold in a bottle shaped like a pregnant woman, a traditional and not-so-subtle hint from a mother-in-law to her son's new bride to get busy making grandchildren. Or create your own liqueur by soaking damania in vodka and blending with honey and spices.

dandelion leaf

dandelion

Botanical Name: *Taraxacum officinale*
Part of Plant: leaf
Aroma: herbaceous – a touch bitter
Planetary Ruler: Jupiter
Element: air
Sexuality: masculine
Blends: **Strew:** Prayer Feet.

Qualities: Dandelion seems perfectly designed to channel and disperse spiritual energies of the Earth. A floret of broad, succulent leaves gathers and funnels rain and dew into the thick, deep taproot, while its ball of delicate flowers disperses with the slightest breeze. Fresh leaves are eaten in salads and dried leaves bring a fairy energy to herb blends.

dandelion root

Botanical Name: *Taraxacum officinale*
Part of Plant: root
Aroma: earthy – woodsy with a warm edge
Planetary Ruler: Jupiter
Element: air
Sexuality: masculine
Blends: **Smudge:** Masculine Manna. **Immersant:** Trance.

Qualities: The roasted root of dandelion can serve as a coffee alternative with a grounding energy. Burned, it's slightly visionary and has a roasty aroma.

dill

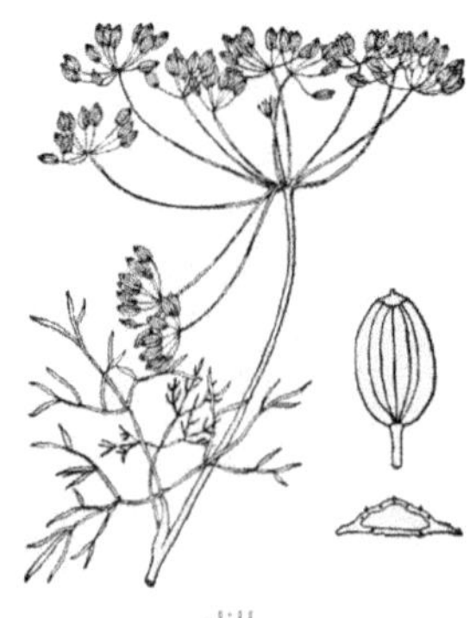
dill

Botanical Name: *Anethum graveolens*
Part of Plant: leaf, seed
Aroma: sharp – mildly pungent
Planetary Ruler: Mercury
Element: fire
Sexuality: masculine
Blends: **Potpourri:** Happy Mix.

Qualities: One of the carminative seeds, dill is cleansing and uplifting, yet the seeds make some folks frisky. The aroma of fresh leaves can induce sleepiness.

Dittany of Crete (hop marjoram)

Dittany of Crete

Botanical Name: *Origanum dictamnus*
Part of Plant: leaf
Aroma: sharp – oregano-like
Planetary Ruler: Venus
Element: water
Sexuality: feminine
Blends: **Offering:** Passages, Spirit Food.

Qualities: Although Dittany of Crete looks and smells like a typical garden herb, it has a greater reputation. The smoke aids in the manifestation of disembodied spirits. Inhaled, it assists in astral projection. Keep fumitory or asafoetida on hand, however, just in case the spirits you manifest are not the kind you thought you were inviting.

dragon's blood

Botanical Name: *Daemomorops draco*
Part of Plant: resin
Aroma: resinous – a bit acrid
Planetary Ruler: Mars, Pluto
Element: fire
Sexuality: masculine
Blends: **Offering:** Tree Temple. **Element:** fire.

Qualities: The resin of a palm tree, dragon's blood usually comes in hard, dense, red clumps that are difficult to measure in quantities unless ground. It adds a potency and sense of action to blends and is associated with empowered dying.

elder, black

Botanical Name: *Sambucus nigra*
Part of Plant: flower, wood
Aroma: floral – with a honey edge; woody – with a pleasant sharpness
Planetary Ruler: Venus
Element: water
Sexuality: feminine
Blends: **Smudge:** Beltane or Summer Solstice Bonfire. **Offering:** Passages. **Potpourri:** Mellow Yellow.

elder

Qualities: The elder tree has a great magical history. It brings protection, insight and initiation.

fennel

Botanical Name: *Foeniculum vulgare*
Part of Plant: seed

Aroma: sharp – pungent, spicy
Planetary Ruler: Mercury
Element: fire
Sexuality: masculine
Blends: **Strew:** Positive Space. **Potpourri:** Happy Mix

Qualities: This is another of the carminative seeds that absorb negativity. Fennel helps instill courage and action and it has an attractive crescent shape with grooves.

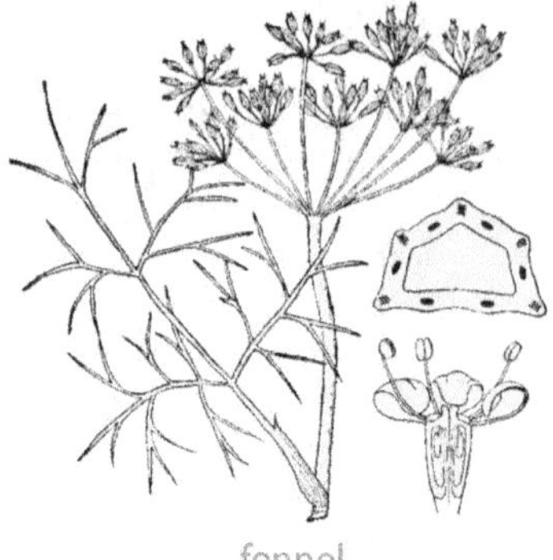

fennel

frankincense

Botanical Name: *Boswellia thurifera*
Part of Plant: resin
Aroma: resinous – light with a touch of spice and sweet
Planetary Ruler: Sun
Element: fire
Sexuality: masculine
Blends: **Smudge:** Masculine Manna. **Offering:** Sun Salutation, Tree Temple. **Element:** fire.

Qualities: Frankincense is the classic offering with a light, lovely smoke that represents the Sun and human intellect. The aroma sharpens intellectual perception while it lifts us out of linear thought. Inhaled, it deepens the breath and taken in before bedtime it stimulates dreams. The attractive gold resin is also called olibanum, from the Arabic "al-luban."

galangal

Botanical Name: *Alpinia officinalum*
Part of Plant: root
Aroma: earthy – ginger with an evergreen edge
Planetary Ruler: Mars
Element: fire
Sexuality: masculine
Blends: **Offering:** Releasing. **Element:** fire. **Immersant:** Divination & Dream Enhance, Trance.

Qualities: This Southeast Asian root shows up in Thai cooking, psychotropic beverages and Pink Floyd songs. Inhaled or drunk, it stimulates psychedelic visions and lust, which are amplified if the root is soaked in vodka first. A potent dose is useful in breaking old patterns. The leaves have a slight citrus aroma with a strange soapy overtone. Exercise prudence after ingesting this herb. Not for pregnant women or for those under 18.

hops

Botanical Name: *Humulus lupulus*
Part of Plant: flower

Aroma: herbaceous – slightly sour
Planetary Ruler: Pluto
Element: air
Sexuality: masculine
Blends: **Element:** air. **Strew:** Prayer Feet.
Potpourri: Mellow Yellow.

Qualities: Hops is a happy vining plant that makes loads of pale green fluffy flowers known for giving beer its bite. Relaxing to inhale, it's a must in sleep pillows and is also healing to the feet.

hops

hyssop

Botanical Name: *Hyssopus officinalis*
Part of Plant: leaf, flower
Aroma: herbaceous – strong, slightly bitter
Planetary Ruler: Jupiter
Element: fire
Sexuality: masculine
Blends: **Smudge:** Masculine Manna, Solar Purification. **Offering:** Releasing.
Element: fire. **Strew:** Positive Space.

hyssop

Qualities: Hyssop is a powerful temple herb renowned for its ability to strongly purge negativity. Inhaled, it stimulates deep breathing. Purifying to the max, it can even engender sadness at the loss of so much held energy. Taken internally, it'll purge you for sure.

juniper

Botanical Name: *Juniperus communis*
Part of Plant: berry, wood
Aroma: resinous – sharp, evergreen
Planetary Ruler: Sun (Drew)
Element: fire
Sexuality: masculine
Blends: **Smudge:** Solar Purification.
Potpourri: Prosperity.

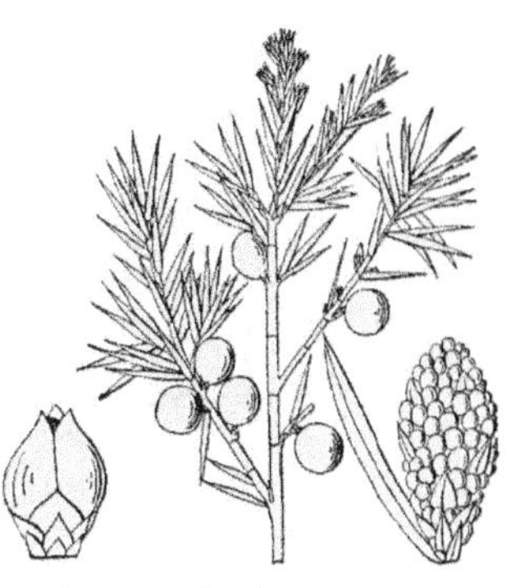

juniper

Qualities: Juniper gives us the classic uplifting evergreen aroma, analogous to cedar, that perfectly captures the element of fire and the energy of the Sun. It's used in the recipes in this book as a berry or essential oil from the wood.

kava kava

Botanical Name: *Piper methysticum*
Part of Plant: root

Aroma: earthy – woodsy with pepper bite
Planetary Ruler: Venus, Pluto
Element: water
Sexuality: feminine
Blends: **Immersant:** Trance.

Qualities: This mildly hypnotic "mystic pepper" makes us tranquil and keeps us alert at the same time. It eases anxiety and promotes insights. In higher doses it encourages psychedelic visions and lust. In Pacifica it is served as a tea relaxant, though some folks like me find the taste quite awful. Kava kava's psychedelic effect becomes stronger if it's prepared with a saturated fat, so make a chocolate milk shake or add a dollop of coconut oil. Do not use it daily. Exercise prudence after ingesting this herb. Not for pregnant women or those under 18.

lavender

Botanical Name: *Lavendula officinale*
Part of Plant: flower
Aroma: floral – herbal
Planetary Ruler: Mercury
Element: air
Sexuality: masculine
Blends: **Potpourri:** Mellow Yellow.

Qualities: Lavender is the herb of romance and happiness.

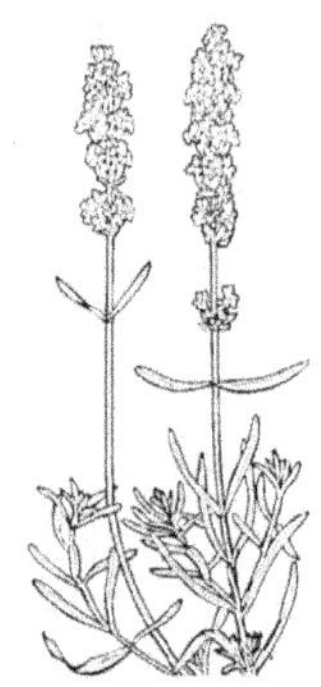
lavender

mandrake

Botanical Name: *Atropa mandragora*
Part of Plant: root
Aroma: earthy – a bit putrid, especially when fresh or dampened
Planetary Ruler: Mercury, Uranus, Pluto
Element: fire
Sexuality: masculine
Blends: **Offering**: Passages. **Immersant**: Aphrodite's Desire, Deep Meditation.

Qualities: Mandrake is powerful psychic plant that induces a deeply meditative state and enhances vivid dream images. It is a central nervous system depressant and should be used with caution and only in small amounts. Not for pregnant women or those under 18.

mugwort

Botanical Name: *Artemisia vulgaris*
Part of Plant: leaf
Aroma: herbaceous – musty, slightly sharp
Planetary Ruler: Moon, Venus, Neptune (Martin et al)
Element: earth
Sexuality: feminine
Blends: **Smudge:** Lunar Purification. **Offering:** Moon Commune. **Inhalant:** Chill Out. **Immersant:** Deep Meditation, Divination & Dream Enhance, Trance.

Qualities: This herb of the Moon is my favorite plant, of course. Even if many herbal experts don't view it as lunar, much of the public, especially female, associate it with the moon. I've watched it turn the silvery undersides of its leaves up toward the Moon and follow it across the sky through the night. Used in acupuncture as moxibustion, mugwort draws energy up and out like the Moon moves the tides. A moxibustion roll, available at Traditional Chinese Medicine outlets, is an easy way to burn mugwort. (It looks like a giant joint!) Inhaled, mugwort enhances psychic abilities and causes prophetic dreams. As a member of the Artemisia plant family, which includes the wormwood of absinthe fame, mugwort should not be partaken of by pregnant or nursing women.

mugwort

muira pauma

Botanical Name: *Liriosma ovata*
Part of Plant: wood
Aroma: earthy – woodsy, slightly acrid
Planetary Ruler: unknown
Element: unknown
Sexuality: unknown
Blends: **Immersant:** Aphrodite's Desire.

Qualities: A small Brazilian tree, this frisky plant is stimulating to the libido and the central nervous system and greatly increases skin sensitivity. Often called "potency wood," it's especially effective on men. Soak it in vodka for a love cocktail; add chocolate or coffee liqueur to cover the sharp woody taste.

myrrh

Botanical Name: *Commiphora myrrha*
Part of Plant: resin
Aroma: sweet – strongly musky with a hint of bitter
Planetary Ruler: Moon
Element: water
Sexuality: feminine
Blends: **Smudge:** Feminine Focus, Lunar Purification. **Offering:** Moon Commune, Passages, Releasing, Spirit Food, Tree Temple. **Element:** water. **Inhalant:** Chill Out. **Immersant:** Deep Meditation.

Qualities: Myrrh overrides intellectual analysis and taps into deep feelings. I've seen people burst into tears upon smelling it. It has a most fascinating way of expanding when burned, producing volumes of extremely lively, turbulent smoke that spiritual entities are deeply drawn to. It is purifying and healing, an excellent and often overlooked smudge and an extremely heartfelt offering. Myrrh empowers other herbs when combined with them and provides a lush low aroma note to resin blends. All this richness of spirit comes from a spiny knotted shrub from the Arabia and Africa deserts.

patchouli

Botanical Name: *Pogostemon patchouli*
Part of Plant: leaf
Aroma: herbaceous – warm, sweet and musky with slight spice
Planetary Ruler: Pluto
Element: earth
Sexuality: feminine
Blends: **Element:** earth. **Immersant:** Aphrodite's Desire.

Qualities: Renowned for inspiring thoughts of romance, patchouli doubles as a prosperity aid. The love and money herb also promotes relaxation of inhibitions and expectations. Its musky aroma adds a warm undertone in blends.

pennyroyal

Botanical Name: *Mentha pulegium*
Part of Plant: leaf
Aroma: sharp – minty
Planetary Ruler: Mars (Drew)
Element: fire
Sexuality: masculine
Blends: **Strew:** Prayer Feet.

Qualities: Pennyroyal is not only stimulating and strengthening to the feet when walked upon, it also strongly discourages bugs. Not to be inhaled or ingested by pregnant women.

pepper

Botanical Name: *Piper nigrum*
Part of Plant: berry
Aroma: spicy – sharp, hot
Planetary Ruler: Mars (Drew)
Element: fire
Sexuality: masculine
Blends: **Potpourri:** Happy Mix.

Qualities: Pepper absorbs negativity and purifies while strengthening and sharpening other herbs it's blended with. It comes in pink, white and black.

poplar (Balm of Gilead)

Botanical Name: *Commiphora opobalsamum*, in US *Populus balsamifera*
Part of Plant: bud
Aroma: basalmic – sharp, resinous, minty
Planetary Ruler: Venus

Element: water
Sexuality: feminine
Blends: **Offering:** Passages, Spirit Food. **Element:** water. **Potpourri:** Prosperity.

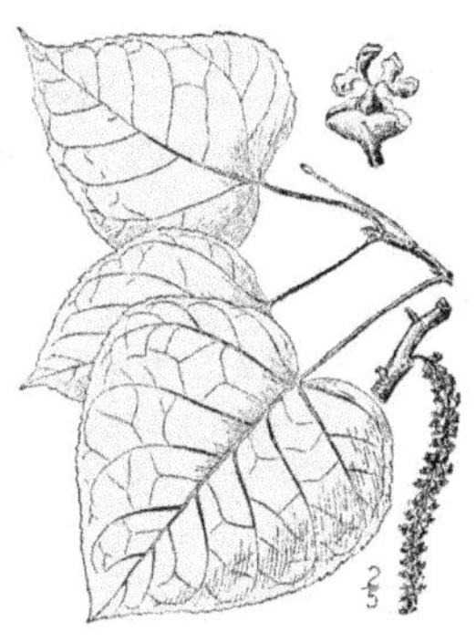
poplar

Qualities: The sap of the rare *Commiphora opobalsamum* tree is the famed Biblical Balm of Gilead's active ingredient. Because it's seldom exported from the Middle East, in the U.S., the resin is extracted from poplar tree buds. Among its more magical attributes is assisting the spirit's release from the body after death. It has a dense, sharp, slightly sweet smell that many entities find appealing.

rosemary

Botanical Name: *Rosmarinus officinalis*
Part of Plant: leaf
Aroma: herbaceous – sharp, resinous
Planetary Ruler: Sun
Element: fire
Sexuality: masculine
Blends: **Smudge:** Beltane or Summer Solstice Bonfire, Solar Purification. **Offering:** Passages, Releasing. **Inhalant:** Mind Sharpen.

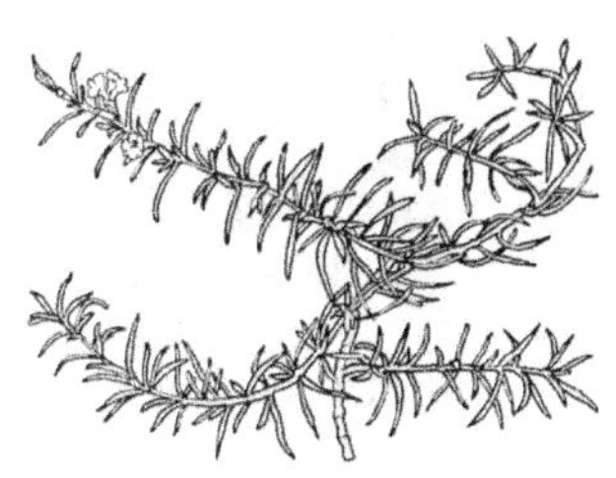
rosemary

Qualities: A resinous purifier similar to sage, rosemary goes a step further to sharpen the mind, heighten memory and encourage compassionate love.

sage, clary

Botanical Name: *Salvia sclarea*
Part of Plant: leaf
Aroma: herbaceous – sweet, sharp and floral at the same time
Planetary Ruler: Mercury (Drew)
Element: air
Sexuality: masculine
Blends: **Immersant:** Aphrodite's Desire, Trance.

clary sage

Qualities: The essential oil of clary sage promotes feelings of euphoria and confidence in one's intuition.

sage, white

Botanical Name: *Salvia apiana* (Frontier Herbs)
Part of Plant: leaf
Aroma: herbaceous – sharp, herbal

white sage

Planetary Ruler: Venus
Element: earth
Sexuality: feminine
Blends: **Smudge:** Solar Purification.

Qualities: Sage's botanical name, salvia, comes from the Latin salvere, meaning "to be saved," which reveals the genre's reputation as sacred herbs. White sage is native to the southwestern U.S. and northwestern Mexico. Why it's assigned as feminine and connected to Venus, though, I haven't a clue, as it acts totally masculine solar to me. Its pale smoke is strongly vertical, ascending directly and quickly almost straight up in a column. The smudge is intensely purifying, sometimes so much as to leave the aura vulnerable. White sage that grows wild is rarely as high quality or even the same plant as that grown by herb farmers.

sandalwood

Botanical Name: *Santalum album*, now endangered, and *Santalum ellipticum*
Part of Plant: wood
Aroma: woody – spicy with warm undertones
Planetary Ruler: Moon (Drew)
Element: water
Sexuality: feminine
Blends: **Smudge:** Feminine Focus, Lunar Purification. **Offering:** Moon Commune, Passages, Tree Temple.

Qualities: A tree of East Asia, ground sandalwood is a staple of Hindu temple incense. Yellow sandalwood has a softer, deeper smell than the red, but they look great blended together and a bit of red brings out the sweetness of the yellow. The warm and slightly resinous aroma blends disparate aromas together. The smoke is protective and purifying, while the aroma sharpens the mind. It can be used with tree resins to tone down the sweetness. Inhaling the aroma promotes alertness and brings one closer to the divine.

scullcap, Virginian

scullcap

Botanical Name: *Scutellarias lateriflora*
Part of Plant: leaf, flowers
Aroma: herbaceous – musty, a bit bitter
Planetary Ruler: Saturn, Pluto
Element: water
Sexuality: feminine
Blends: **Immersant:** Deep Meditation.

Qualities: A strongly tranquilizing herb, scullcap works not by sedation but by soothing the nerves.

The herbal "chill pill" is a powerful nervine that calms the neurological reactions that fuel anxiety and neurotic behavior.

slippery elm

slippery elm

Botanical Name: *Ulmus fulva*
Part of Plant: inner bark
Aroma: woody – lightly spicy
Planetary Ruler: Saturn
Element: air
Sexuality: feminine
Blends: **Smudge:** Beltane or Summer Solstice Bonfire. **Offering:** Releasing.

Qualities: Slippery elm does more than soothe throats with a mucilage-rich tea. It also brings pleasantness to all communication and stops the circulation of gossip.

St. John's wort

St. John's wort

Botanical Name: *Hypericum perforatum*
Part of Plant: leaf
Aroma: herbaceous – a bit bitter
Planetary Ruler: Sun
Element: fire
Sexuality: masculine
Blends: **Smudge:** Beltane or Summer Solstice Bonfire. **Offering:** Sun Salutation. **Immersant:** Divination & Dream Enhance.

Qualities: This plant of the Sun boasts yellow flowers that bloom at the height of summer and release red sap when crushed. As a nervine, it soothes and promotes optimism. Inhaled it can cause dreams of a true love or life's path.

sweet woodruff

sweet woodruff

Botanical Name: *Asperula odorata*
Part of Plant: leaf
Aroma: herbaceous – with a touch of vanilla
Planetary Ruler: Venus, Mars (Drew)
Element: fire
Sexuality: masculine
Blends: **Smudge:** Beltane or Summer Solstice Bonfire.

Qualities: This gentle woodland herb associated with Beltane and protection also imparts a unique flavor to May Wine.

thyme

thyme

Botanical Name: *Thymus vulgaris*
Part of Plant: leaf
Aroma: herbaceous – sharp, lightly resinous
Planetary Ruler: Venus
Element: water
Sexuality: feminine
Blends: **Smudge:** Feminine Focus.

Qualities: Thyme is a gentle yet persistent purifier and protector.

valerian

Botanical Name: *Valeriana officinalis*
Part of Plant: root
Aroma: earthy – musty, somewhat fetid
Planetary Ruler: Venus (Drew)
Element: water
Sexuality: feminine
Blends: **Smudge:** Feminine Focus. **Element:** earth. **Inhalant:** Chill Out.

valerian

Qualities: Valerian is the original relaxant that valium imitates in both name and action. Grounding and stabilizing, it purifies and protects. While the foliage and flowers are quite sweet smelling, the root aroma is worse than old socks that cats find irresistible.

vervain, blue

blue vervain

Botanical Name: *Verbena officinalis*
Part of Plant: leaf
Aroma: herbaceous – grassy, a touch sharp
Planetary Ruler: Venus
Element: earth
Sexuality: feminine
Blends: **Smudge:** Beltane or Summer Solstice Bonfire, Feminine Focus. **Element:** earth. **Immersant:** Deep Meditation. **Strew:** Perimeter Protection, Positive Space.

Qualities: The "herb of grace" is like a mellow version of hyssop, just as purifying but not as punishing. It's a mild little plant that boasts a powerful impact and strong protective energy.

vetivert

Botanical Name: *Vetiveria zizanoides*
Part of Plant: root
Aroma: earthy – warm and rich
Planetary Ruler: Venus (Drew)

Element: earth
Sexuality: feminine
Blends: **Element:** earth. **Immersant:** Aphrodite's Desire.

Qualities: Another love and money plant, vetivert's earthy aroma is integral to many perfume blends. It's most commonly available as an essential oil.

vetivert

wild lettuce

Botanical Name: *Lactuca virosa*
Part of Plant: root
Aroma: earthy – strongly sweet, musky
Planetary Ruler: Moon
Element: water
Sexuality: feminine
Blends: **Smudge:** Lunar Purification. **Offering:** Moon Commune. **Immersant:** Deep Meditation, Divination & Dream Enhance.

wild lettuce

Qualities: Wild lettuce contains a mild opium-like substance that induces a meditative state and enhances vivid dream images. This is a very funky plant, mild on the outside and wild on the inside. Concentrates are widely available on the internet. Exercise prudence after ingesting this herb. Not for those under 18.

wood betony

Botanical Name: *Betonica officinalis*
Part of Plant: leaf
Aroma: herbaceous – grassy with a musky edge
Planetary Ruler: Venus, Jupiter
Element: fire
Sexuality: masculine
Blends: **Smudge:** Beltane or Summer Solstice Bonfire, Masculine Manna. **Offering:** Releasing. **Immersant:** Divination & Dream Enhance. **Strew:** Perimeter Protection.

wood betony

Qualities: Betony has strongly protective and purifying qualities, plus the interesting ability to help repair quarrels. A fabulous herb!

yerba mate

Botanical Name: *Ilex paraguayensis* (Frontier Herbs)
Part of Plant: leaf
Aroma: herbaceous – grassy with tea-like undertones

Planetary Ruler: unknown
Element: unknown
Sexuality: unknown
Blends: **Immersant:** Aphrodite's Desire.

Qualities: The lusty and stimulating leaf of this South American tree is the favored herb of Carnival, the mate tea that makes the dancers and drummers go go go on the streets and in the sheets!

yerba santa

Botanical Name: *Eriodictyon californicum* (Drew)
Part of Plant: leaf
Aroma: herbaceous – strongly musty, a bit resinous
Planetary Ruler: unknown
Element: unknown
Sexuality: unknown
Blends: **Smudge:** Solar Purification.

Qualities: An excellent and overlooked herb, yerba santa is one of my favorites. The Mexican "herb of the saints" is called the "portable temple" because of its all-purpose ability to purify, protect and provide a conduit to the divine. It's perfect when paired with white sage.

lung buffer herbs

for immersant blends

coltsfoot

Botanical Name: *Tussilago farfara*
Part of Plant: leaf
Aroma: herbaceous – warm, vanilla, mildly spicy
Planetary Ruler: Venus
Element: water
Sexuality: feminine

Qualities: When used as a tea, candy or smoke, coltsfoot can counter coughs and encourage tranquility.

horehound

Botanical Name: *Marrubium vulgare*
Part of Plant: leaf
Aroma: herbaceous – spicy, a touch licorice
Planetary Ruler: Mercury
Element: air
Sexuality: masculine

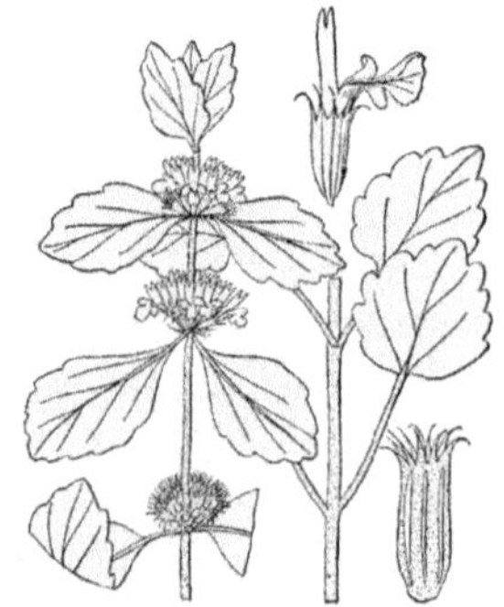
horehound

Qualities: When it's fresh, horehound makes terrific candy. The mucilage-rich tea and smoke loosens chest congestion and soothes frayed lung tissue.

lungwort

Botanical Name: *Sticta pulmonaria* (Frontier Herbs)
Part of Plant: leaf
Aroma: herbaceous – mild
Planetary Ruler: unknown
Element: unknown
Sexuality: unknown

Qualities: Lungwort is all-around helpful to the lungs.

mullein, great

mullein

Botanical Name: *Verbascum thapsus*
Part of Plant: leaf
Aroma: herbaceous – a bit musty
Planetary Ruler: Saturn
Element: fire
Sexuality: Feminine

Qualities: A very fuzzy plant, mullein is high in mucilage and soothing to the lungs.

pleurisy root

Botanical Name: *Asclepias tuberose* (Frontier Herbs)
Part of Plant: root
Aroma: earthy – mild
Planetary Ruler: unknown
Element: unknown
Sexuality: unknown

Qualities: Another herb that is nurturing and soothing to the lungs.

ceremony safety herbs

asafoetida

Botanical Name: *Ferula foetida*
Part of Plant: root resin
Aroma: foul – garlic gone very bad
Planetary Ruler: Pluto
Element: fire
Sexuality: masculine

Qualities: Toss this powder on hot charcoal and all spirits, malevolent or otherwise, will go away. So will all people and other living things. Asafoetida is extremely foul smelling and should be stored in a disposable plastic container inside a glass jar.

camphor

Botanical Name: *Cinnamonum camphora*
Part of Plant: resin
Aroma: resinous – sharp, eucalyptus-like
Planetary Ruler: Moon
Element: water
Sexuality: feminine
Blends: **Inhalant**: Mind Sharpen.

Qualities: The aroma of camphor can help bring focus to someone who's overly emotional or libidinous, disassociating, spacing out, or otherwise going over the edge. It's sort of like psychological smelling salts. The essential oil from *Cinnamonum camphora* is more common than bulk camphor, which comes as beige granules. Apply oil to a cotton ball and pass it beneath the nose. Or saturate organic matter with oil, place it on embers and inhale the aroma. Avoid the small camphor tablets used in Hindu temple and wedding poojas, and the camphor found in drugstores. These are made of synthetic camphor.

fumitory

Botanical Name: *Fumaria officinalis*
Part of Plant: leaf
Aroma: herbaceous – mild
Planetary Ruler: Saturn
Element: earth
Sexuality: feminine

Qualities: Fumitory dispels negative energy with a swift kick in the rear, leaving positive spiritual energies mostly intact. It's also good for calming down groups who get cranky and mutinous.

fumitory

rock salt

salt

Chemical Name: sodium chloride
Aroma: varies
Planetary Ruler: Sun
Element: fire
Sexuality: masculine
Blends: **Potpourri:** Happy Mix.

Qualities: There is a wonderland of salt in an amazing array of colors and flavors, with sources ranging from seawater to mountains. Conventional table salt is usually made of processed halite. How boring! Epson salt is magnesium sulfate; don't use it for ceremonial salt.

salt

Salt is used indoors to purge negativity and purify. For potpourris, a chunky salt is needed. It will be labeled as chunk, coarse, crystal, grosso or grinder salt. Salt from evaporated seawater is widely available. But seek and ye shall also find coarse pink salt from the Himalayas, brownish pink Hawaiian sea salt rich in volcanic minerals, even sea salt smoked to a deep black.

notes on male & female attributes

In cultural lore, plants are considered to be male or female. Plants that embody strength and active expression, have hot aromas and are dark in appearance, are seen to be male. Female plants are those that encapsulate beauty and receptive expression, have cold aromas and are light colored generally.

Designations for a plant's sexuality mostly agree with those in **A Wiccan Formulary and Herbal** by A.J. Drew. Exceptions are noted and refer to texts or websites in Resources.

notes on planets, elements & deities

Other cultural assignments include planetary and elemental correspondences, and affinities with certain deities.

In general, air is associated with the east and intellect, ideas and invention. Earth is associated with the north and stability, sustenance and wisdom. Fire is associated with the south and spirit, passion and creativity. Water is associated with the west and emotion, communication and the subconscious.

Planetary correspondences generally match those given by Paul Beyerl in **A Compendium of Herbal Magick**. Exceptions are noted and refer to texts or websites in Resources.

Elemental correspondences mostly agree with those in **A Wiccan Formulary and Herbal** by A.J. Drew. Exceptions are noted and refer to texts or websites in Resources.

notes on botanical names

My source for most botanical names is M. Grieve's **A Modern Herbal**. The specific variant of an herb often makes a great deal of difference. For instance, there are hundreds of acacias, but ***Acacia nilotica*** is what makes gum Arabic.

notes on herb images

All herb images other than those from QuickArt® are courtesy of USDA, NRCS. 2008. The PLANTS Database (http://plants.usda.gov, 11 March 2008). National Plant Data Center, Baton Rouge, LA 70874-4490 USA.

All Britton & Brown illustrations were scanned by Omnitek, Inc.

angelica
QuickArt® images © Wheeler Arts. All rights reserved. www.wheelerarts.com

basil
QuickArt® images © Wheeler Arts. All rights reserved. www.wheelerarts.com

bay laurel
QuickArt® images © Wheeler Arts. All rights reserved. www.wheelerarts.com

calendula
QuickArt® images © Wheeler Arts. All rights reserved. www.wheelerarts.com

caraway
Britton, N.L., and A. Brown. 1913. An illustrated flora of the northern United States, Canada and the British Possessions. Vol. 2: 659. Courtesy of Kentucky Native Plant Society.

chamomile, common
Britton, N.L., and A. Brown. 1913. An illustrated flora of the northern United States, Canada and the British Possessions. Vol. 3: 517. Courtesy of Kentucky Native Plant Society.

coltsfoot
Britton, N.L., and A. Brown. 1913. An illustrated flora of the northern United States, Canada and the British Possessions. Vol. 3: 531. Courtesy of Kentucky Native Plant Society.

coriander
Britton, N.L., and A. Brown. 1913. An illustrated flora of the northern United States, Canada and the British Possessions. Vol. 2: 647. Courtesy of Kentucky Native Plant Society.

corn
Hitchcock, A.S. (rev. A. Chase). 1950. Manual of the grasses of the United States. USDA Miscellaneous Publication No. 200. Washington, DC. 1950.

dandelion
QuickArt® images © Wheeler Arts. All rights reserved. www.wheelerarts.com

dill
Britton, N.L., and A. Brown. 1913. An illustrated flora of the northern United States, Canada and the British Possessions. Vol. 2: 634. Courtesy of Kentucky Native Plant Society.

Dittany of Crete
QuickArt® images © Wheeler Arts. All rights reserved. www.wheelerarts.com

elder, black
USDA NRCS. Wetland flora: Field office illustrated guide to plant species. USDA Natural Resources Conservation Service. Provided by NRCS National Wetland Team, Fort Worth, TX.

fennel
Britton, N.L., and A. Brown. 1913. An illustrated flora of the northern United States, Canada and the British Possessions. Vol. 2: 643. Courtesy of Kentucky Native Plant Society.

fumitory
Britton, N.L., and A. Brown. 1913. An illustrated flora of the northern United States, Canada and the British Possessions. Vol. 2: 146. Courtesy of Kentucky Native Plant Society.

hops
Britton, N.L., and A. Brown. 1913. An illustrated flora of the northern United States, Canada and the British Possessions. Vol. 1: 633. Courtesy of Kentucky Native Plant Society.

horehound
Britton, N.L., and A. Brown. 1913. An illustrated flora of the northern United States, Canada and the British Possessions. Vol. 3: 110. Courtesy of Kentucky Native Plant Society.

hyssop
Britton, N.L., and A. Brown. 1913. An illustrated flora of the northern United States, Canada and the British Possessions. Vol. 3: 140. Courtesy of Kentucky Native Plant Society.

juniper
Britton, N.L., and A. Brown. 1913. An illustrated flora of the northern United States, Canada and the British Possessions. Vol. 1: 66. Courtesy of Kentucky Native Plant Society.

lavender
QuickArt® images © Wheeler Arts. All rights reserved. www.wheelerarts.com

mugwort
QuickArt® images © Wheeler Arts. All rights reserved. www.wheelerarts.com

mullein, great
Britton, N.L., and A. Brown. 1913. An illustrated flora of the northern United States, Canada and the British Possessions. Vol. 3: 173. Courtesy of Kentucky Native Plant Society.

poplar
Britton, N.L., and A. Brown. 1913. An illustrated flora of the northern United States, Canada and the British Possessions. Vol. 1: 588. Courtesy of Kentucky Native Plant Society.

rosemary
QuickArt® images © Wheeler Arts. All rights reserved. www.wheelerarts.com

sage, clary
Britton, N.L., and A. Brown. 1913. An illustrated flora of the northern United States, Canada and the British Possessions. Vol. 3: 131. Courtesy of Kentucky Native Plant Society.

sage, white
QuickArt® images © Wheeler Arts. All rights reserved. www.wheelerarts.com

scullcap
USDA NRCS. Wetland flora: Field office illustrated guide to plant species. USDA Natural Resources Conservation Service. Provided by NRCS National Wetland Team, Fort Worth, TX.

slippery elm
USDA NRCS. Wetland flora: Field office illustrated guide to plant species. USDA Natural Resources Conservation Service. Provided by NRCS National Wetland Team, Fort Worth, TX.

St. John's wort
Britton, N.L., and A. Brown. 1913. An illustrated flora of the northern United States, Canada and the British Possessions. Vol. 2: 533. Courtesy of Kentucky Native Plant Society.

sweet woodruff
QuickArt® images © Wheeler Arts. All rights reserved. www.wheelerarts.com

thyme
QuickArt® images © Wheeler Arts. All rights reserved. www.wheelerarts.com

valerian
Britton, N.L., and A. Brown. 1913. An illustrated flora of the northern United States, Canada and the British Possessions. Vol. 3: 286. Courtesy of Kentucky Native Plant Society.

vervain, blue
Britton, N.L., and A. Brown. 1913. An illustrated flora of the northern United States, Canada and the British Possessions. Vol. 3: 95. Courtesy of Kentucky Native Plant Society.

vetivert
Hitchcock, A.S. (rev. A. Chase). 1950. Manual of the grasses of the United States. USDA Miscellaneous Publication No. 200. Washington, DC. 1950.

wild lettuce
Britton, N.L., and A. Brown. 1913. An illustrated flora of the northern United States, Canada and the British Possessions. Vol. 3: 318. Courtesy of Kentucky Native Plant Society.

wood betony
Britton, N.L., and A. Brown. 1913. An illustrated flora of the northern United States, Canada and the British Possessions. Vol. 3: 128. Courtesy of Kentucky Native Plant Society.

resources

books ~ web sites

books

A Compendium of Herbal Magick
By Paul Beyerl
Publisher: Phoenix Publishing

In this well-organized and lengthy guide to the ceremonial use of herbs, the first section is an overview of herbal methods, the middle section is a fairly concise dictionary of 330 magical herbs with 100 illustrations, and the final section features more information on magical uses of herbs, along with astrological, deity and planetary correspondences.

Cunningham's Encyclopedia of Magical Herbs
by Scott Cunningham
Publisher: Llewellyn

A good book on magical herbs once you parse out the abundant folklore and get to the general qualities of each herb. Features small but helpful drawings.

Magical and Ritual Use of Aphrodisiacs
Magical and Ritual Use of Herbs
Magical and Ritual Use of Perfumes
by Richard Alan Miller
Publisher: Destiny Books

Three excellent books by biochemist and herbalist Richard Alan Miller feature in-depth information on a limited number of very powerful herbs. In addition to tremendous technical details, there's great historical info that is short on folklore and long on verifiable data. Explanations of techniques for herbal preparation and use are drawn from indigenous cultures around the world.

Plants of the Gods
by Richard Evans Schultes & Albert Hoffman
Publisher: Healing Arts Press

Albert Hoffman, the famed inventor of LSD, penned this ethnobotanist's bible about plants that work on the mind with an esteemed biology professor. Contains astounding first-hand information on indigenous cultures around the world with in-depth info on 91 wild herbs, most of which you'll never see in the U.S. Incredible pictures and drawings.

A Wiccan Formulary and Herbal

by A. J. Drew.
Publisher: New Page
An easy-to-use guidebook on herbs covers the full gamut of techniques and contains good info on practical matters like tools. The herbal dictionary is well laid out with surprisingly insightful info, but erratically alphabetized. This great, concise all-around guide is suitable for beginners.

web sites

Frontier

www.frontiercoop.com

This herb supplier's web site features an impressive library on herbs. Click on Our Products and then on Herbs (A to Z)

Wikipedia

www.Wikipedia.com

Wikipedia? For herbs? Yep, it's a great source for basic non-magical information, with color pictures, too. Plant geeks have uploaded all kinds of info from primo sources like the USDA database. All entries list their references and contain additional links; some are super-annotated.

A Modern Herbal

www.Botanical.com

Mrs. M. Grieve's "A Modern Herbal" was first published in 1931 and it was indeed modern then. The entire text has been uploaded to a web site in an easy-to-search format. Much more is known of herbs since this book was written, but the author had a discerning eye for ferreting out reputable folklore. Includes good information on plant habitat and growing habits.

Mountain Rose

www.mountainroseherbs.com

Buried in the order page are links for Contemporary Info (worth digging for) and Folklore Info (which is the M. Grieve text).

SaltWorks

www.saltworks.us

The web site of a supplier of gourmet sea salts and bath salts from around the world has a Gourmet Salt Reference Guide that is a fascinating read.

U.S. Department of Agriculture PLANTS database

http://plants.usda.gov/

The federal government is the ultimate source of non-magical plant info. The easiest way to access the database is to click on Fact Sheets & Plant Guides. You can also search by common or botanical name. Much info is available as pdf files. Great pictures!

index of herbs

s

t

u

v

w

y

z

www.ingramcontent.com/pod-product-compliance
Lightning Source LLC
LaVergne TN
LVHW020656100826
845148LV00012B/2526
* 9 7 8 0 9 8 1 8 4 2 4 0 0 *